TWENTIETH CENTURY
BRASS MUSICAL INSTRUMENTS
IN THE UNITED STATES

by
Richard J. Dundas

Distributed by
Queen City Brass Publications
Box 75054, Cincinnati, Ohio 45275
(A Division of Queen City Publishing, Inc.)

PUBLISHED BY RICHARD J. DUNDAS

ISBN 0-9617093-1-6
First Printing July 1986
Revised Edition 1989

Library of Congress
Catalog Card Number 86-90264

DISTRIBUTED IN THE UNITED STATES
BY QUEEN CITY BRASS PUBLICATIONS
Box 75054, Cincinnati, Ohio 45275
(A Division of Queen City Publishing, Inc.)

PRINTING AND BINDING IN THE UNITED STATES
BY SHARP OFFSET PRINTING
Rutland, Vermont 05701

FRONT COVER PHOTO: A group of instruments owned by the author.

PHOTOGRAPHS: Most of the photographs were contributed by the manufacturers. Instrument photos not otherwise credited are from the author's collection.

TABLE OF CONTENTS

ACKNOWLEDGEMENTS

Since a large share of the material in this book was adapted from catalogs, brochures and news releases provided by instrument manufacturers and distributors, footnote references to each source would take up almost as much space as the text and be of no interest to most readers. Instead, I prefer to express my appreciation in this form to all of the companies represented for their help in supplying printed material and photographs and authorizing its use.

Additional recognition should be given to the following people for their contributions of otherwise unavailable information in letters and conversations: David Monette, Jerome Callet, Donald Benge, Zig Kanstul, Reynold Schilke, Irma Calicchio, Lawrence Sansone, Merle O. Johnson (E. K. Blessing Company), Kevin Bergner (Yamaha Musical Products), Donald G. Close and Jacob Khan (Boosey & Hawkes Edgware plant), Donald E. Getzen (DEG Music Products), Lloyd Farrar (American Musical Instrument Society) and Robert Sheldon (Smithsonian Institution).

Martin Krivin's dissertation, "A Century of Wind Instrument Manufacturing in the United States: 1860-1960," and Lyndesay Langwill's *An Index of Musical Wind Instrument Makers* have enabled me to include names, dates and locations that even the present officers of the companies concerned could not supply because of lack of records or, in the case of companies now out of business, no contact person was available. Both authors graciously permitted me to use information from their works.

The music dealers magazine, "Music Trades," provides excellent coverage of new products and corporate changes which alerted me to the necessity for follow-up contacts to the manufacturers concerned for up-dated information on instruments and management changes.

Photographs in the section on early instruments were provided through the courtesy of Stuart and Lillian Caplin from their collection at The Center for Musical Antiquities.

Richard J. Dundas
Rutland, Vermont

INTRODUCTION

Coach horn *(Center for Musical Antiquities photo)*

EARLY
BRASS INSTRUMENTS

Many fine books have been written about the early history and development of musical instruments — from prehistoric times through the Middle Ages, the Renaissance and the Baroque period. In recent years music scholars have begun to focus their attention on the latter part of the eighteenth and the nineteenth century. This was the most productive period in the entire history of brass instrument development.

It began with the crude natural horns limited to the harmonic tones of a single key. These instruments were usually made in some variation of a straight tube with a flared bell. The ones designed to make high pitched sounds were short enough in length to be left straight like the fanfare trumpet and coach horn when their usefulness was enhanced by the flashy appearance of a straight horn. When used as a signal device by hunters and military units, a four foot long tube would be an encumbrance and had to be coiled or folded.

The next refinement was the addition of crooks and tuning bits of assorted sizes to vary the sounding length of the natural horns. While this permitted the use of horns in some concert pieces it limited the composers and performers to the harmonic tones of a single key at any given time. The task of creating a horn with a continuously variable sounding length and a resulting chromatic scale was simple enough in principle and had been known to instrument makers since sometime in the seventeenth century. Slide trumpets and sackbuts or primitive trombones had this capability. However, the practical problem of fabricating metal tubes that would slide together freely and not leak air was not fully mastered until the nineteenth century.

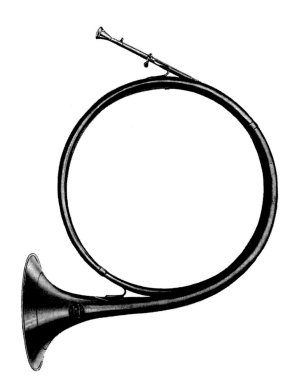

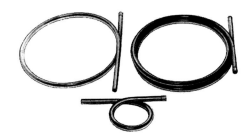

Modern replica of hunting horn with tuning crooks
(Gebr. Alexander photo)

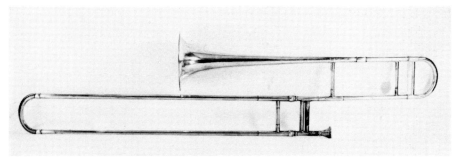

Slide trombone *(Center for Musical Antiquities photo)*

Early in the nineteenth century tone holes operated by keys were added to bugles and to an upright horn known as an ophicleide to fill in the missing notes between harmonic tones. This scheme was satisfactory enough to demonstrate the great musical potential of horns with a full scale and composers began to take advantage of this new flexibility of horns to add new voices or tonal colors to operas, orchestral works, court music and military music.

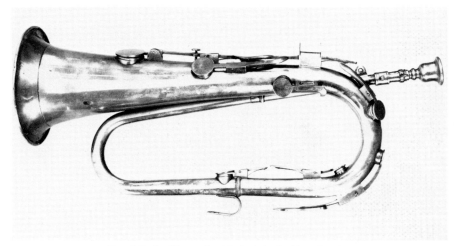

Keyed Bugle *(Center for Musical Antiquities photo)*

Ophicleide *(Center for Musical Antiquities photo)*

The European instrument makers at this time were also experimenting with a variety of valve systems to direct sound waves through tubes of different lengths to achieve a chromatic scale with the robust quality of a natural horn and the flexibility of a keyed instrument. The two most satisfactory systems that finally evolved from these experiments were the rotary valve and the piston valve which supplanted keyed tone holes on horns and have continued unchanged to the present time to provide the basic design for the entire family of brass instruments, except for the slide trombone.

Cornopean with stolzel valves

Bass horn with Vienna valves
(Center for Musical Antiquities photo)

Tenor horn with Berlin valves
(Center for Musical Antiquities photo)

Rotary valve cornets with early variations of airway designs and valve operating mechanisms *(Center for Musical Antiquities photo)*

Ruggerio *(Naples)* **rotary valve trumpet with rotary key change valve**

Modern versions of early design rotary valve flugelhorns

Piston valve C cornet with extension tubes and slide for Bb and A

During the nineteenth century brass instrument design and fabrication was of such widespread interest that the annual trade expositions in most countries featured an instrument competition. Prizes and ratings by judges were so cherished by the manufacturers that they imprinted the list of awards to a given model on the bell along with their name, address and company hallmark.

Museums and private collections are filled with excellent examples of these early and transitional instruments but once brass instruments reached a high level of refinement and uniformity of design to give them the capability of producing sound in any pitch, timbre or velocity required by composers of the period, they ceased to be of interest to musicologists, curators and collectors.

In the twentieth century brass musical instruments have been generally regarded as durable, dependable machines and are no longer considered novel or unique in any way except to a small percentage of the estimated two million people throughout the world who are currently playing them. The great mass of student and amateur brass players continue to play whatever brand and grade of instrument they were given as small children. The majority of the instruments were selected by parents with the advice of a local music dealer, school band director or music teacher. Professional players, on the other hand, are constantly testing and experimenting with instruments to achieve the unique performance characteristics needed for their work. Modern brass instruments are so standardized in design, appearance and intonation that only a professional player, after extensive testing, can distinguish one brand or grade from another. However, in spite of the uniformity of instrument design and performance, most players acquire an affinity for their own horn and a strong brand loyalty. In many cases this loyalty is to a brand name popularized by the endorsement of a famous player or a respected teacher. They seldom know anything about the manufacturer's history or contributions to instrument development.

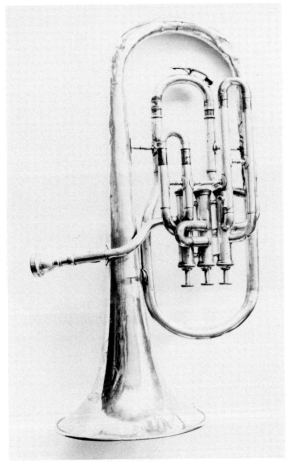

Piston valve Eb alto horn

VARIETIES OF MODERN BRASS INSTRUMENTS

The variety of brass instruments currently used in the United States by bands, symphony orchestra, chamber groups or pop music groups includes trumpets in Bb, C, D, Eb, F, G and high A, Bb and C; single, double and triple French horns in F, Eb and Bb; trombones in tenor and bass Bb, F and Eb; baritone horns and euphoniums in Bb; tubas and sousaphones in EEb, BBb and CC. The Bb and Eb cornets, the Eb alto horn and the F/Eb mellophone, formerly standard band instruments, are not used much at present but the flugelhorn and the valve trombone are enjoying a new vogue with pop music groups. Some standard instruments like the mellophone, baritone and tuba have been modified in shape to give a uniform horizontal bell-front appearance to suit marching bands. Other brasses, such as the pocket cornet and herald trumpet, have been compressed or stretched out for special effects and novelty acts.

Some manufacturers have reduced the variety of their product line in order to meet sales demands for a particular model. Several companies now concentrate on student instruments and one or two produce only professional trumpets and cornets. Some have merged and produce several distinctive lines in the same factory. Others have stopped manufacturing and concentrate on distributing imported brands. Others have acquired foreign companies with plant facilities to produce a segment of their product line, like baritone and bass horns.

Information about manufacturers, unique features of the instruments and technical specifications of various models is not available in periodicals of general circulation or existing reference books. Instrument dealers have a limited number of brochures containing this information and some of it is available in advertisements and feature stories in music journals but it requires considerable research for a musician to learn much about his recent model instrument and it is virtually impossible to find information pertaining to an instrument that is 20 to 50 years old or out of production.

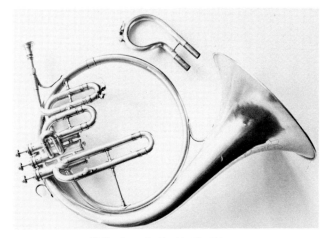

Mellophone in F with Eb slide

Flugelhorn *(Getzen photo)*

Valve trombone *(Getzen photo)*

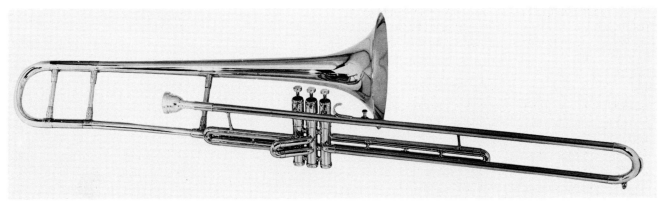

Triumphal or herald trumpet and bass trumpet *(Selmer photo)*

PURPOSE OF THIS BOOK

This book is a collection of available information about the history and characteristics of the brass instruments manufactured or distributed extensively in this country in the twentieth century. The manufacturers and distributors have graciously contributed and authorized publication of illustrations and descriptions of their products. The resulting publication should provide a comprehensive guide to modern brass instruments — elaborate enough in detail to give an instrument fancier as much information as he needs and concise enough to enable an owner to estimate the value of an unfamiliar brand of instrument.

Any attempt to make comparisons or qualitative judgements about the instruments described here would be pointless and lead to endless controversy. Every instrument that has ever been made is regarded by its designer and manufacturer as the best available for its cost and intended use and these claims are enthusiastically endorsed by a substantial number of satisfied users of each model. On the other hand, many professional players insist that no production models are satisfactory and have to mix components from several makers to get a customized instrument that embodies the features they need.

However, the information will never be completely or fully up-to-date. In the first six months of 1985 alone, four manufacturers exhibited prototypes of new model professional trumpets. In the past five years at least four major brands have gone out of production and several distinguished obsolete brands have been reintroduced. Some companies that were famous for the quality of their brasses in the early part of the century have changed ownership and product lines so often that nothing remains of the original company except the label attached to a different type of product. Early historical information and catalogs for these companies have been lost or destroyed and were not available to the author. This material will have to be added later from contributions by readers or further research by the author.

Many readers will find errors and omissions in this guide to modern brass instruments and they are encouraged to send corrections or additional information to the author for inclusion in later revised editions.

Richard J. Dundas
31 North Street Extension
Rutland, Vermont 05701

GEBR. ALEXANDER MAINZ

The Alexander Company is the oldest brass instrument manufacturer in West Germany. It was founded in Mainz in 1782 by Franz Ambrose Alexander and has been owned and managed by his descendants in an unbroken succession to the present time. Alexander instruments are distributed in the United States exclusively by the Getzen Company and are of particular interest to professional musicians with highly specialized requirements. They are one of the two American-represented companies currently producing a full line of cornets, trumpets and flugelhorns in both rotary and piston valve models. The French horn section of their catalog shows not only the conventional single and double horns but also natural horns, hand horns with crooks to play in any key, single descant horns for high baroque parts in several keys, double descant horns and a triple horn encompassing the high F range as well as the normal B♭ and F ranges. Their alto, tenor and baritone horns are made in both the Wagner oval shape with rotary valves and in upright models with piston valves. The Alexander tubas are all rotary models with four to six valves.

1753—1802
Franz Ambros Alexander

1787—1826
Philipp Alexander

1803—1872
Kaspar Anton Alexander

1838—1926
Franz Anton Alexander

1849—1897
Georg Philipp Alexander

1879—1916
Philipp Alexander

1873—1913
Anton Alexander

1904—1971
Philipp Alexander

1935
Anton Alexander

1948
Hans-Peter Alexander

Owner/Managers of the Alexander Company from 1782 to the present time *(Alexander photo)*

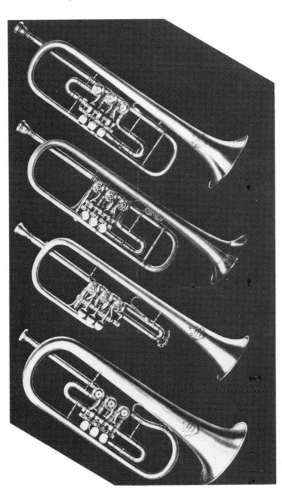

Rotary valve trumpets *(Alexander photo)*

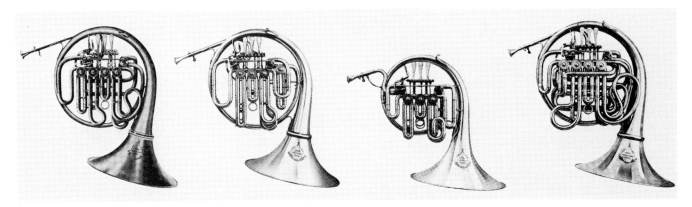

Some of the French horns in the Alexander line *(Alexander photo)*

Wagner tuben *(Alexander photo)*

Some of the tubas in the Alexander line *(Alexander photo)*

VINCENT BACH

Vincent Bach was born in Austria in 1890 and received his mechanical engineering diploma in 1910. While studying engineering in the technical school he was also developing his proficiency as a trumpeter through private instruction. He emigrated to the United States in 1914 and held positions as first trumpet in the Boston Symphony and the Diaghilev Ballet Orchestras. Next, he was bandmaster of the 306th U.S. Army Field Artillery Band and director of an Army bugle school.

After leaving the Army in 1918, Bach began to manufacture mouthpieces and by 1924 had expanded into design and manufacture of high quality trumpets and cornets, strongly resembling the French Besson which was his personal choice as an artist. He added trombones to his product line in 1928. As more players learned about the quality of Bach mouthpieces and instruments the demand for them increased and Bach moved his original one-lathe shop to two more spacious locations in New York City before opening a new modern factory in Mount Vernon, N.Y., in 1953. This facility could have produced and sold far more than the 5000 instruments made by Mr. Bach but his output consisted largely of custom models developed through extensive experiments in design and metallurgy. Bach's engineering background enabled him to prepare mandrels, models, working drawings and technical records of his designs so that any of them could be accurately duplicated without trial and error or repeated experimentation. This extensive variety of components enabled Bach to produce combinations of bell, mouthpiece and bore to suit the requirements of any artist. Even today, when most manufacturers offer no more than three variations of a particular model (medium, medium-large and large bore), the Bach "Stradivarius" Bb trumpet is sold in 51 alternate combinations of bell, mouthpipe and bore.

Vincent Bach *(Selmer photo)*

New York Bach "Stradivarius" cornet bell label

Bach "Stradivarius" trombone *(Selmer photo)*

3

Bach "Stradivarius" Bb trumpet *(Selmer photo)*

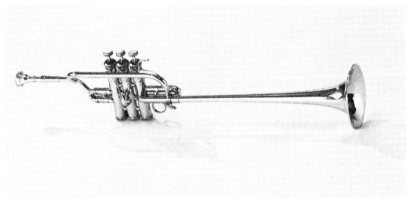

Bach "Stradivarius" piccolo trumpet *(Selmer photo)*

Bach "Stradivarius" flugelhorn *(Selmer photo)*

In 1961 Bach transferred design, manufacturing and sales responsibilities to the Selmer Corporation but continued his experimental work as a consultant for the new owners of his company. His work for Selmer included redesigning their Bundy brand instruments and developing a mass-produced variation of the "Stradivarius" line marketed as the Bach "Mercedes I" at an intermediate price. He also developed a Selmer "Signet" and Bach "Mercedes II" series priced slightly above basic student instruments. His last design project was the Bach "Stradivarius" French horn, which never got into production.

Vincent Bach died on January 8, 1976, the day before the New York Brass Conference for Scholarships had scheduled a "Salute and Tribute to Vincent Bach" as the high point of their annual spring meeting. The program, under the direction of Dr. Charles Colin, was quickly converted to a memorial service of mammoth proportions, with about 500 professional and advanced student brass players participating in the musical tribute to one of the most influential and respected designers of the twentieth century.

New York Bach Bb trumpet with 1st valve slide ring added

Mt. Vernon Bach "Stradivarius" trumpet *(Selmer photo)*

Model 182 Bach "Stradivarius" flugelhorn *(Selmer photo)*

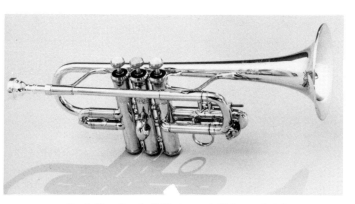

Bach "Stradivarius" Eb trumpet *(Selmer photo)*

Many musicians claim that there has never been a bad Bach instrument and the New York and Mount Vernon brasses are particularly treasured because each one is believed to have been created personally by the master. However, they are not all equally desirable for all players because the New York and Mount Vernon models were designed for the original artist-purchaser with many specialized features that would not be suitable for all players. Extensive testing and comparison of bell, bore and mouthpipe combinations should precede purchase of a Bach "Stradivarius" but the "Mercedes I" and "Mercedes II" models all have a medium large bore and a standard bell and mouthpiece.

Bel Canto Trumpets

The Bel Canto trumpet was named for its ability to project a "tender, pure, expressive singing style, characterized by a clear, focused legato and a strident marcato," according to Severinsen-Akright, Inc., the designers and manufacturers. The association of trumpeter "Doc" Severinsen and designer Richard Akright follows a long-standing tradition of collaboration between artists and manufacturers that began in Europe with J. B. Arban and Antoine Courtois, in the U.S. in the 1860's with Patrick Gilmore and Samuel Graves and included Herbert L. Clarke and Frank Holton, Thomas King and Henderson White, and other artist/designer teams in later years. In each case the artist wanted a custom-designed, hand-made instrument for personal use. When one was developed with superior qualities the decision was made to share these improvements with other players through limited, carefully supervised duplication personally checked by the artist.

To suit differing requirements of the other artists, additional models were produced with variations in bore size, bell pipe and leadpipe characteristics. The Bel Canto is now made in two Bb variations of Mr. Severinsen's model and a large bore C trumpet for symphony players. Designs are now being tested for an Eb/D trumpet and a Bb cornet.

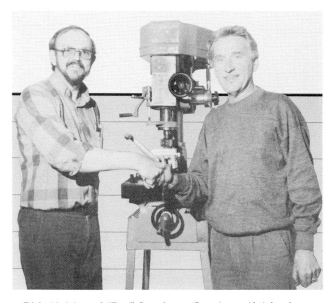

Dick Akright and "Doc" Severinsen *(Severinsen-Akright photo)*

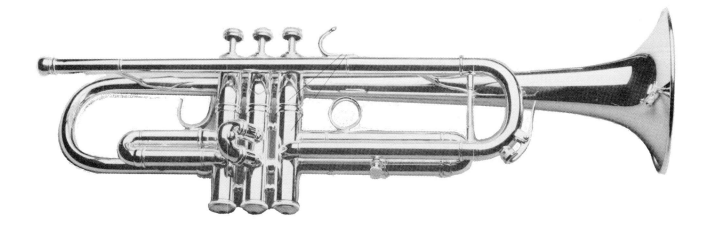

Bel Canto Bb trumpet *(Severinsen-Akright photo)*

BENGE

The founder of the Benge Musical Instrument Company, Elden Benge, was born July 12, 1904, in Winterset, Iowa, and moved to Glendale, California, about 1916. He began to play a cornet at age 9 and studied with Harold Mitchell who got him started on his professional career in Pasadena, California, with a theater orchestra. He progressed to a first trumpet position with the Detroit Sympany Orchestra for two years and moved on to the Chicago Symphony Orchestra for a ten year period as an associate of Edward Llewellyn and Renold Schilke.

Like most symphony players at that time, Benge used a French Besson trumpet and considered it the best available instrument but wanted to experiment with further refinements. He tried to get his designs adopted by an established manufacturer but was unable to get anyone to risk the expense of retooling. In order to test his ideas he set up a home workshop and eventually learned how to fabricate, assemble and finish all of the parts needed to make professional trumpets, although he had no prior metalworking experience.

His first instrument was made about 1935 and he gradually increased production to about 225 a year by 1960. The early handmade instruments from the Chicago factory are as prized by collectors as the New York and Mt. Vernon model Bach trumpets and cornets. From 1960 to 1971 the company was managed by Benge's son, Donald, and he expanded production to about 1100 units per year. It was during this time that Claude Gordon, a famous orchestra leader and studio trumpeter, became associated with the Benge Company as an artist-consultant—an association which continued until 1983. Like the elder Benge, Claude Gordon was devoted to the French Besson and his initial designs for improvements were also based on the Besson. The external resemblance is still evident in the latest model Benge trumpets but their playing characteristics have been refined to suit the specialized requirements of a wide range of professional players. Among dance orchestra, studio and recording artists the Benge trumpet has been more popular than any other brand for many years. Recently, several of the larger manufacturers have made effective inroads on this segment of the market with custom designed instruments but Benge's loss in this area has been offset by sustantial gains in the adoption of their C, E*b* and four-valve piccolo B*b* trumpets by symphony and ensemble players.

Elden Benge 1904-1960 *(Benge family photo)*

Claude Gordon was an artist-consultant for the Benge Company until 1983 and more recently has developed a new model trumpet for the Selmer Corporation *(Benge photo)*

Benge factory in Anaheim, California *(Benge photo)*

The Benge Company has never deviated from its original purpose of making only high quality professional trumpets, cornets and flugelhorns. They have not developed an intermediate or student line of instruments and they have resisted the temptation to expand into production of French horns, trombones and harmony brasses. Schilke Music Products and Callichio Musical Products are the only other American companies currently limiting production to professional grade cornets, trumpets and flugelhorns.

Donald Benge sold the company in 1971 and its promotion and distribution operations are now managed by King Musical Instrument Company. Until 1983, the two companies had completely separate design and manufacturing facilities—Benge in a small modern factory in Anaheim, California, and King half way across the country in one of the world's largest brass instrument factories in Eastlake, Ohio. King produces a full line of their own label brasses, including some models that compete with Benge, in addition to marketing Benge trumpets and Armstrong flutes. In 1983, Benge production facilities were moved to the King plant in Ohio to be more efficiently integrated with the parent company. King designers enhanced the Benge line by producing a new series of "Symphonic" trumpets and trombones for symphony orchestra and ensemble players. Fortunately for the Benge craftsmen in California who did not choose to move to Ohio, Boosey & Hawkes decided to resurrect the French Besson trumpet and make it in that area. Ironically, many of the same workers and designers who perpetuated and refined the F. Besson trumpet for Benge now have an opportunity to make it under the original label as redesigned for Boosey & Hawkes by Zig Kanstul.

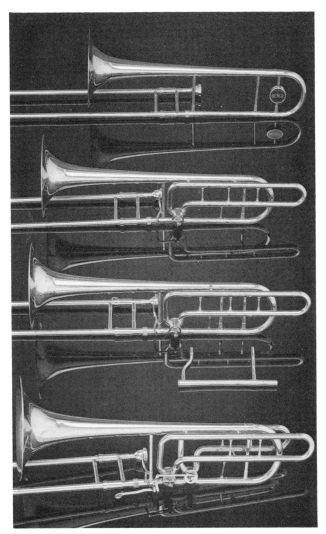

Benge "Symphonic" Trombones *(King photo)*

Benge Symphonic Trumpets "Leonore" *(King photo)*

Besson

Gustave Besson 1820-1874 *(Besson photo)*

Besson Bb trumpets *(Besson photo)*

Gustave Besson was born in 1820 in Paris and began learning instrument manufacture at the age of 10 as an apprentice to Dujarier. Dujarier was one of the first French brass manufacturers to experiment with two and three piston value instruments. Besson began to work independently on instrument designs by the time he was 14 years old and founded his own company in Paris when he was 18. Besson's products became popular in France and won awards at the Paris Exhibition beginning in 1844 but his sales were limited by heavy competition from older and more distinguished firms like Adolphe Sax, Courtois and Gautrot. By 1857 his instruments were in such great demand in England that he established a branch factory in London and devoted much of his time to its operation. The Paris factory continued to operate under the direction of his wife and daughters, Cecilia and Martha.

After Besson's death in 1874, the active management of both plants was supervised by Besson's daughter, Martha, and her husband, a French diplomat named Fontaine. In 1894 the Fontaine-Bessons sold the London branch of the firm and concentrated in the Paris factory on improving existing types of wind instruments and developing new types capable of performing with full color and authenticity the works of such contemporary composers as Wagner, Gounod, Saint Saens, Tchaikowski, Vincent d'Indy and others. Mrs. Fontaine-Besson was given many honors at exhibitions and testimonials from famous musicians and composers for the quality of the instruments that she developed. The instruments based on her designs are stamped with both the F. Besson name and an ornate monogram with the Fontaine-Besson initials entwined.

In 1908 both Mr. and Mrs. Fontaine-Besson died within a few weeks of each other and the management of the Paris company was inherited by their youngest daughter. She appears to have also inherited her parents' and grandparents' interest and talent in instrument making because the family name continued for a third generation to dominate competitions and awards for quality instruments.

The personal history of the Besson family and details about the operation of the Paris branch of the Besson Company are difficult to trace after 1910 but French Besson trumpets and cornets remained the first choice of most of the world's great artists until the 1960's. The emergence of the Besson Company in London as a major supplier of professional and student instruments in the British Isles, Canada and the United States diminished the separate identity of the French Besson company but provided excellent marketing and distribution facilities by featuring the custom-made French Besson as the top of their combined line.

The Besson Company's London branch not only produced cornets and trumpets in large quantities but took over major responsibility for production and marketing of the famous Besson family-designed harmony brasses with a compensating valve system. D. J. Blaikley's invention of the compensating valve system in 1874 provided the most ingenious, practical and enduring solution to the faulty intonation problem inherent in piston valve designs. This system was protected by patents but a further deterrant to modification and adoption by other manufacturers was the expense and difficulty of making valve assemblies with additional air passages and attached valve tubes. Besson offered this system as an extra-cost option on the professional grade instruments. Both the French and English Besson instruments were fabricated on steel mandrels and this made them unusually uniform compared to other 19th century brasses. During the early part of the 20th century, Besson engineers pioneered in the development of special techniques for bending tubes without stretching or cracking the metal. Their efficient manufacturing methods, coupled with the popularity of Besson instruments, put such demands on production capacity that they moved frequently to larger quarters until finally settling into the Edgware factory in 1924.

Sales of Besson instruments in the United States have been effectively promoted by major distributors like Carl Fischer and C. Bruno & Son and by manufacturers like Buescher who sold Besson-made harmony brasses in the 1970's and acted as agents for Besson compensating valve instruments. Boosey & Hawkes have distributed Besson instruments in the U.S. since establishing a marketing division in New York after World War II.

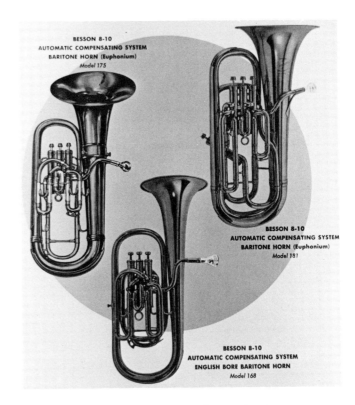

Besson baritone horns *(Besson photo)*

Besson recording bass and tuba *(Besson photo)*

10

The French Besson trumpets and trombones apparently went out of production sometime in the 1960's and the latest models appeared to have been made in the Couesnon factory because they shared design details with the Couesnon line. During the 1970's the English Besson label was supplanted by Boosey & Hawkes labels and modified designs. In 1983 Boosey & Hawkes announced the resurgence of the F. Besson trumpet to be made in a new factory in Los Angeles, California. The new F. Besson line consists of the "Meha" model B*b* in two bore sizes and the "Meha" C trumpet in three bore sizes, each with three interchangeable lead pipes. The "Brevette" model B*b* is offered in two bore sizes.

Besson trombones *(Besson photo)*

Bell label on new model F. Besson trumpet showing prizes and honors earned by the early models *(Boosey & Hawkes photo)*

Turn-of-the-century English Besson cornet with accessories.

Blessing

Handcrafted Musical Instruments Since 1906

Emil K. Blessing 1873-1954 *(Blessing photo)*

As early as 1901, Emil K. Blessing was building brass instruments on a small scale and in 1906 he founded the E. K. Blessing Company to make valve assemblies for other manufacturers. He also produced complete cornets, trumpets and trombones for other companies. Vincent Bach was one of his early instrument customers as well as a life-long close friend and continued to buy valve assemblies from Blessing while concentrating on development of the infinite variety of mouthpipe and bell designs that characterize modern Bach instruments.

Blessing was the first manufacturer to use octagonal outer valve casings, caps and buttons and his designs may have influenced other manufacturers like Schilke and Getzen to use that shape for caps and buttons. All of the early 20th century manufacturers were attempting to produce domestic instruments that could compete with the French Bessons. It is not surprising that the professional grade Blessing "Super Artist" line and many other early American models shared a common silhouette with the French Besson. Eventually, the American manufacturers developed original designs that have remained fairly constant up to the present time.

Throughout its entire history, Blessing has been a family-owned company. Blessing's sons, Karl and Fritz, managed the office and sales departments until their retirement in the late 1960's and his daughter's husband, Merle O. Johnson, worked in all phases of the company from 1949 until he purchased it in 1964 and has served as president since that time. Their eldest son, Randy Johnson, is now active in the company's marketing division and may eventually become the third generation head of E. K. Blessing Company.

Blessing factory in Elkhart, Indiana *(Blessing photo)*

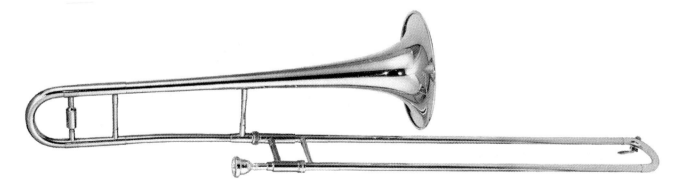

XL series trombone *(Blessing photo)*

Early Blessing cornet with double leadpipe
(Priscilla Douglas Collection)

Merle O. Johnson, president of E. K. Blessing Company since 1964
(Blessing photo)

In the 1920's and 30's, Blessing produced a full line of brasses but cut back for a period of time to concentrate on meeting heavy demand for their popular cornets, trumpets and trombones. Gradually, they have expanded their product line to include the full array of marching brasses; three grades of cornets, flugelhorns, trumpets and trombones; two grades of French horns and a full line of concert band harmony brasses.

Blessing instruments are sold in thirty-two foreign countries and are available at practically every dealership in the U.S. Their designs are up-to-date and the instruments are very competitive with other American and imported brands for quality and price.

"Artist" double French horn *(Blessing photo)*

"Masterpiece" Bb trumpet *(Blessing photo)*

XL series Flugelhorn *(Blessing photo)*

BOOSEY & HAWKES
(MUSICAL INSTRUMENTS) LTD
Deansbrook Road, Edgware, Middlesex HA8 9BB
Tel. 01-952 7711

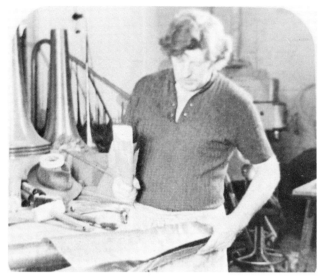
Hand forming tuba bell. Finished bell in background *(B & H photo)*

The Boosey & Hawkes Company was founded in 1792 as a bookstore by Thomas Boosey, great-great grand-father of Leslie Boosey who was president of the company from 1919 to 1930. The musical branch began with imported manuscripts and scores and by 1816 was a major music publisher specializing in operas. Publishing and promoting vocal music continued to be a major interest of the company well into the twentieth century but their involvement with brass instrument manufacturing began in 1868 with the purchase of Distin & Company when the owner, Henry Distin, emigrated to Philadelphia. This company was founded by John Distin in the early nineteenth century and is credited with many significant contributions to the design and refinement of brass instruments. Because of this acquisition of a complete factory, fully equipped and employing the best available designers, technicians and supply sources, Boosey was able to enter the brass instrument business on a par with Besson and the other established firms rather than working up from a modest beginning.

The Hawkes branch of the company was founded by William Henry Hawkes in 1865 at 33 Soho Square, London, in partnership with Jules Riviere. Riviere was a bandmaster and orchestra conductor and Hawkes was a cornet soloist with the Scots Fusilier Guards and State Trumpeter to Queen Victoria. Their original interest was in music publishing but the firm soon developed extensive reed and brass instrument manufacturing facilities. After relocating to Leicester Square in 1876, brass instrument manufacture was expanded by Hawkes' son, Oliver, who was with the firm until his death in 1919. From 1919 until the merger with Boosey in 1930, the company was managed by Geoffrey and Ralph Hawkes from the Denman Street facilities acquired in 1895.

Finish shaping bells on mandrel in lathe *(B & H photo)*

The Boosey & Hawkes Company was based at the Boosey offices at 295 Regent Street but continued to use the Denman Street plant and a factory built in 1924 in the London suburb of Edgware. The Edgware factory has been damaged by fire twice and rebuilt and improved each time to handle constantly increasing production demands. Boosey & Hawkes shared the Edgware plant and many production designs with Besson & Company until the mid-1970's. At that time Boosey & Hawkes purchased all rights to Besson & Company in order to unify products, marketing and management services for the combined companies.

Hawkes & Son flugelhorn made at Denman Street, Piccadilly Circus

14

Boosey & Hawkes Edgware factory with giant drum *(B & H photo)*

Boosey & Hawkes currently manufactures and distributes a full line of brass instruments in at least two grades: "Sovereign" for the professional grade and "Regent" for student instruments. An intermediate grade labled Besson "Imperial" is offered in some types of instruments.

In 1982, Boosey & Hawkes American division president, Jon Crist, announced a joint venture with Zig Kanstul to reintroduce the famous French Besson trumpet. Kanstul managed the Olds Band Instrument plant in Fullerton, California, for 18 years and was in charge of production at the Benge Musical Instrument Company in Anaheim, California, until it was moved to the headquarters of its parent company, King Musical Instruments, in Eastlake, Ohio.

It is particularly appropriate that the man who most recently headed the company that was dedicated to perpetuating the French Besson design and playing characteristics in Benge trumpets now has the opportunity to produce a modern version of the original French Besson for marketing by Boosey & Hawkes, who acquired rights to it with their purchase of the British Besson Company many years ago but allowed production to lapse in favor of their own label professional models. The French Besson is now produced in a new factory near Los Angeles, California, but still carries the original label, "F. Besson, Paris" or "F. Besson, Paris-France," depending on the bore size.

Boosey & Hawkes cornet, trumpet and flugelhorn *(B & H photo)*

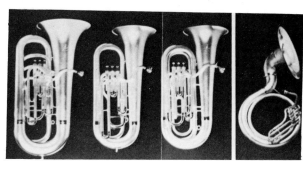

Variety of Boosey & Hawkes bass horns *(B & H photo)*

F. Augustus Buescher established his band instrument factory in Elkhart, Indiana, in 1888 after working for the C. G. Conn Company and operating an instrument repair business. As a designer and instrument maker, Buescher specialized in saxophones but had a broad enough background to build valved brasses as well. By 1900 his factory was large enough to produce a full line of saxophones, from soprano to the relatively rare bass, and a full line of brasses that included cornets, trumpets, mellophones, valve trombones, baritone horns, upright basses and helicons. Before the end of the first decade of the twentieth century, Buescher's production was up to about 3,000 instruments per year and continued to grow at a gradual rate for the next twenty years. In 1928, Buescher took over the Elkhart Band Instrument Company and for the next thirty years used the Elkhart label for intermediate and student grade instruments.

The Buescher Band Instrument Company was acquired by the Selmer Corporation in 1963 but continued to produce instruments under the Buescher label until the late 1970's. During this time the professional grade cornets, trumpets and harmony brasses were completely eliminated from the product line, leaving only the student grade "Aristocrat" made by Buescher and marketed by Selmer. In purchasing Buescher, Selmer also acquired distribution rights to the Besson harmony brasses with their unique compensating valve system. Now, even the Buescher "Aristocrat" is off the market and the Besson line is merged with Boosey & Hawkes instruments distributed by them from their U.S. branch office.

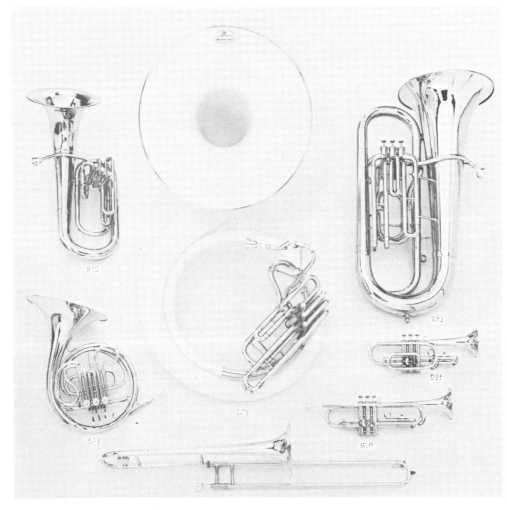

Buescher line of brass instruments in 1972 (Selmer photo)

BURBANK TRUMPET COMPANY

Donald E. Benge and Zig Kanstul with Burbank pocket cornet and flugelhorn *(Burbank photo)*

When the King Musical Instrument Company moved the Benge factory to Eastlake, Ohio, in 1983, most of the employees elected to remain in California and continue working for the production manager, Zig Kanstul, in a new company that he established. Mr. Kanstul's association with the Benge Company began in 1952 as a part-time consultant setting up the factory in Burbank and moving with it to Los Angeles under King ownership. After the Benge Company moved to Ohio, Mr. Kanstul reopened the same Burbank factory that he set up thirty years earlier to develop his own line of Burbank trumpets and a new F. Besson line for Boosey & Hawkes.

In 1984 he persuaded Donald E. Benge to join him in operation and management of the new company. This development brings Mr. Benge back into a business that he grew up in and successfully managed from 1960 to 1971. In the intervening thirteen years so much of his time was needed in other areas of interest that he had to give up his activities in the musical instrument industry. Once he was back into active participation in trumpet manufacturing, Mr. Benge was able to reassert the Benge family philosophy of small volume, high quality instrument production employing highly skilled workmen, individual testing of each instrument and design modifications recommended by a large number of professional players who have an almost proprietary interest in Benge instruments.

It was this responsiveness to the needs of trumpet players during the 1960's that led Mr. Benge to develop a number of new model trumpets, a pocket cornet and a flugelhorn. These models have been perpetuated in the Burbank line and augmented by new design piccolo trumpets that are highly rated by professional players The latest additions to the Burbank line are the 900 and 601 series Bb and C trumpets. Although priced below the original hand crafted Star series, the new models are designed for professional use.

Burbank "Star" series trumpets *(Burbank photo)*

Calicchio

The founder and sole owner of the Calicchio Musical Instrument Company, Domenick Calicchio, was born in Rome on September 13, 1901, and died in Los Angeles in 1979. Until the age of 17 he lived in orphanages in Rome and Milan where he received vocational training in the manufacture and repair of brass instruments. For the next seven years he worked for an uncle in Rome as a tool and die maker. In 1925, he emigrated to the United States and settled in New York City. He worked in machine shops and instrument repair shops before starting his own instrument repair business. That led to the design and custom fabrication of mouthpieces and trumpets which became his lifetime career. In New York from 1928 to 1947 he concentrated on perfecting his New York model basic B*b* trumpet design but after moving to Los Angeles he began to experiment with designs and prototypes for a variety of other instruments, including slide trumpets, trombones, tubas and double-bell horns. The major emphasis in his work was the improvement of mouthpiece and leadpipe designs. His approach to experimentation was, of necessity, by trial and error because he was not a trained scientist or engineer. Instead, he had the practical advantage of being a master metal craftsman due to his early training and years of experience as a repairman, machinist and tool and die maker. Instead of basing his experimental designs on laboratory accoustical tests or physics theories, his ideas for instrument modification came from the reports of performance tests by the host of professional trumpet players who were his ardent supporters in a mutual quest for the perfect

Dominick Calicchio 1901-1979 *(Calicchio photo)*

trumpet. This ideal could only be achieved on an individual basis because players requirements and idiosyncracies vary too much for any instrument to suit them all equally well.

While other designers like Benge, Bach and Schilke shared his desire to make the perfect trumpet, they were professional players and concentrated on the instrument features that were ideal for their own use, with variations to suit their colleagues. Since Calicchio was not a musician, he was much more sensitive to the requirements of his customers and completely unbiased in the design of his instruments.

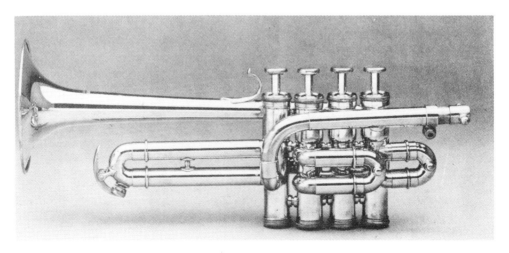

Calicchio piccolo trumpet *(Calicchio photo)*

Most Calicchio trumpets are made-to-order and delivery time averages about three weeks. All parts are hand-made in the Calicchio shop except for braces, water keys, slide rings and hooks, which are purchased. Production has been limited to about three trumpets per week even though the current work force could build as many as seven a week. Deliberately limiting production permits a continuation of the original policy of careful attention to detail and perfection of fit and finish which has always characterized Calicchio instruments. The major share of the production work has been done by the master and a staff of about three "apprentices" whose long experience with the company would qualify them as master instrument makers in any other firm. Calicchio's three daughters have taken care of the financial and administrative details for years and had such thorough early training in all phases of construction and finishing that Irma has been able to serve as General Manager since 1977.

Future plans for the Company call for expansion of the product line to include slide trumpets, C trumpets, three- and four-valve piccolo trumpets, pocket trumpets and a flugelhorn in addition to the basic Bb trumpet. Calicchio holds a patent on an adjustable mouthpiece that permits changing rim, cup and backbore in seconds and this has been so popular that production of this item will probably be increased in the future.

Interchangeability of bell and leadpipe is one of the distinctive features of the Calicchio trumpet. The stock designs consist of four different bells and a choice of thirty different leadpipes in each of three bore sizes. After choosing one of the 120 possible bell and leadpipe combinations, the purchaser can have the bell replaced once and the leadpipe changed twice without charge at the shop within thirty days after delivery. No other manufacturer in the United States offers this kind of customizing and opportunity for further modification as an integral feature of the original purchase price of an instrument.

Current line of Calicchio brasses *(Calicchio photo)*

JEROME CALLET

Jerome Callet is a self-taught trumpet player whose unusual approach to embouchure development has resulted in world-wide recognition as an expert in high and low register tone production. His book, *Trumpet Yoga*, illustrates his methods for developing an effective range from double pedal C to triple high C. He has been teaching and conducting clinics and master classes in New York, Germany and Switzerland for the past thirteen years to promote his methods.

His early training as a machinist enabled him to experiment with mouthpiece designs and over a period of years he developed a selection of mouthpieces to complement his embouchure theories and to improve the performance of many different types of players. His custom mouthpieces are designed to provide quicker response, better pitch control and greater ease in the upper register with good tone and endurance.

Callet's involvement with instruments began with sixteen years in sales for Benge and was followed by nine years of work with Callicchio. For the past six years he has been working on his own designs and has sold about 600 Callet Custom trumpets—many of them to famous players. By having the basic fabrication done under contract to his specifications in a modern factory, Callet is able to custom tune and adjust the bells and lead pipes to produce the best possible response at all sound levels and throughout a five octave range.

Callet Custom Bb and C trumpets are available in medium large, large and super large (.472″) bore. He also has an Eb/D trumpet and a flugelhorn on the market.

Jerome Callet adjusting trumpet leadpipe. Mouthpiece lathe in background *(Bill Spilka photo)*

Jerome Callet adjusting trumpet bell *(Bill Spilka photo)*

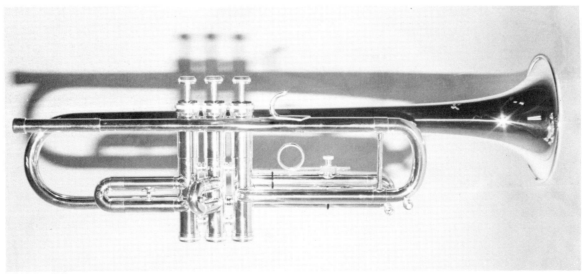

Callet trumpet *(Bill Spilka photo)*

 CONN

The C. G. Conn Company must be considered the undisputed giant of the brass instrument industry. It started earlier than any other company now in existence, moved rapidly and aggressively into large scale production and strong promotion of its products and has held a preeminent position for both quantity and quality up to the present time. Over the years it has been the outstanding quality of a few of their models, widely regarded as the best available at the time, that has maintained the company's reputation and enabled them to sell vast quantities of very good but not remarkable instruments. These unique characteristics of the Conn Company originated in the personality of the founder and have persisted through several generations of management teams.

The founder, Charles G. Conn, was born in 1844 and had an adventurous career as an officer in the Civil War and considerable experience as a cornet player before getting into the music business. His first product was a patent rubber-rimmed mouthpiece, turned on a primitive lathe in a small shop with three or four employees. In 1875 he began to make brass instruments in this shop and within six years had expanded to over 10,000 square feet of factory space and was employing 84 men. In 1887 he purchased the Isaac Fiske factory in Worcester, Massachusetts, and not only acquired additional factory space but the most advanced designs and the best trained American instrument makers of that time. His headquarters remained in Elkhart but instruments of this period made in the Worcester branch were labeled "Elkhart-Worcester" and are considered superior to the Elkhart product. To further increase production of quality instruments, Conn recruited a group of ten to fifteen French craftsmen from the Distin Company in London. This company had been purchased by Boosey & Company in 1868 and the founder, Henry Distin, had emigrated to Philadelphia where he established an instrument manufacturing and importing business that competed actively with Conn until Conn bought him out.

With very large manufacturing facilities and the best designers and technicians at his command, Conn was able to take full advantage of the late nineteenth and early twentieth century world-wide obsession with community and military band music. When this movement spread to the American public schools, the Conn Company was even better prepared for this vast new market for band instruments by virtue of their established mass-production equipment and well-designed student instrument line.

Double F/Bb French horn *(Conn photo)*

Sousaphone. First model developed for John Phillip Sousa in 1897. Made first fiberglass sousaphone in 1961 *(Conn photo)*

c. 1900 E♭ cornet with C crook. Bell labeled "C. G. Conn, Elkhart, Ind. & New York" denoting purchase from Conn's retail store in New York.

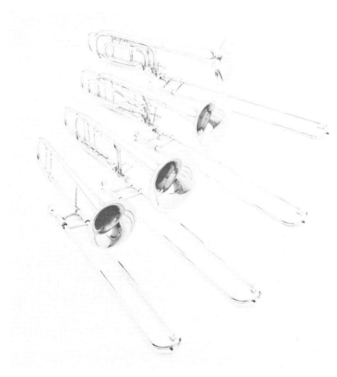

Conn Trombones *(Conn photo)*

After forty years as founder and administrative head of the company, Charles G. Conn sold it in 1915 to Carl D. Greenleaf, who served as president until 1949. During his tenure and up to 1985 under the management of other executive officers, Conn remained independent and a strong competitor in both the mass-market and professional brass instrument lines. In their long and distinguished history, whenever they faced a serious challenge from competitors or public taste, they have managed to respond with product improvements, effective publicity and strong support from their large and loyal dealer network. The most recent examples of this flexibility and responsiveness are found in the 1980 remodeling of their best-selling Conn "Director" student trumpet and the development in 1986 by Conn designers of the new "Heritage" professional B♭ trumpet in medium large and large bore models.

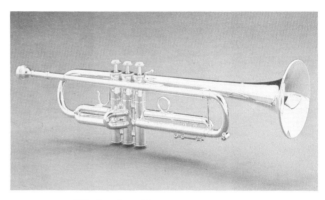

"Heritage" model trumpet *(Conn photo)*

Like most manufacturers, Conn instruments have model names intended to be descriptive or promotional. Among the earliest ones were "Four in One," "Ultimatum" and "Wonder Equa-Tone." The most recent catalog lists "Connstellation," "Artist," "Victor," "Connquest" and "Director" as model names, with model numbers and letters added to the name to designate variations of the model.

In 1985 Conn, King and W. T. Armstrong were purchased by the Swedish conglomerate, Skane-Gripen, and reorganized as United Musical Instruments USA, Inc., under the presidency of Tom Burzcki. Production of Conn, King and Benge brasswinds has been centralized in the Eastlake, Ohio, factory but the distinctive features of the various brand instruments will be retained.

ᴜᴏ couesnon

Couesnon & Cie was founded in 1827 by A. G. Guichard, one of the leading early brass makers, and bought by Gautrot in 1845. Gautrot also achieved recognition for his contributions to brass instrument design and manufacture. In 1881 Gautrot acquired the Triebert woodwind factory which was noted for outstanding oboe design and manufacture. When Amedee Couesnon purchased Triebert & Gautrot in 1883 it was one of the best instrument companies in France. Under Couesnon's management for 48 years, it made even greater progress, winning many prizes and medals for technical improvements. Their ability to produce large quantities of fine instruments under the Couesnon label created a demand from dealers and distributors who wanted good instruments to market under their own label or unmarked. Many such instruments exported to the United States in the early twentieth century were probably made by Couesnon.

By 1911, the firm had expanded to eight factories employing 1000 workers and had become a major source of bugles and band instruments for armies throughout the world. At the same time, Couesnon instruments were a great favorite with the outstanding performers of the period. During this time Couesnon could claim to be the undisputed leader in international sales. Their prominence in the international market continued up to about 1979, with about 60% of production allocated for export. Of this amount, about one-third was sold in the United States where Couesnon instruments have been very popular for at least 50 years. They were distributed in the United States until 1978 by the Fred Gretch Company but are now imported directly by dealers.

Jean Sargueil, President-Director General de Couesnon
(Couesnon photo)

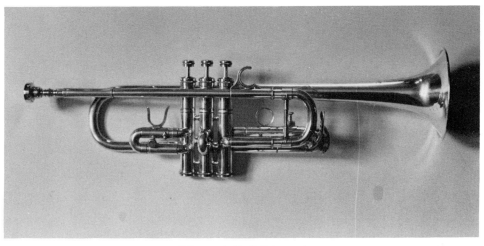

"Monopole Star" C trumpet

To supply the world-wide demand for their instruments, Couesnon consolidated all of its machine tool and production facilities in Chateau-Thiery, a small city on the Marne river, about 50 miles east of Paris. The modern factory complex represents an interesting combination of modern technology and hereditary hand craftsmanship. Some fabrication and assembling processes are highly automated while other operations are still performed in substantially the same way they were developed by the early founders and designers in the nineteenth century.

Couesnon is noted for a number of unusual instrument types and designs. Long before other manufacturers offered professional trumpets in a choice of keys, Couesnon was producing piccolo Bb/A, high F/G, Eb/D, C/Bb and Bb/A combination trumpets in addition to the single key C and Bb models. They are still producing a mellophone and a true French French horn with piston valves and extended stems for left-handed fingering. Their bass horns have design features not currently in production by any other manufacturer—three valves for right hand fingering and one to three additional valves placed for left hand operation.

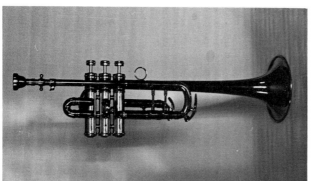

"Monopole Conservatoire" G trumpet with tuning slide extension for key of F

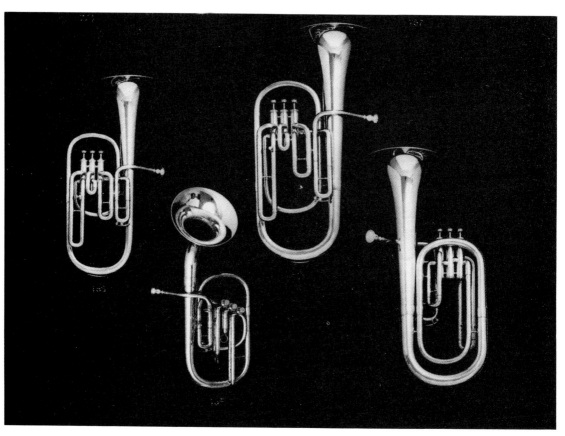

"Monopole Star" Bb/A piccolo trumpet

Couesnon alto and baritone horns *(Couesnon photo)*

Courtois

The Antoine Courtois Company, founded before 1800, is the world's oldest brass maker still in business and claims to have supplied the instruments for Napoleon's musicians. About 1880, the Courtois Company developed the Arban Model cornet that enabled Jean-Baptiste Arban, the famous Paris Conservatoire brass teacher and virtuoso performer, to demonstrate in concerts throughout Europe that the Courtois cornet, as played by him, was a more versatile instrument than the saxhorn or trumpet for orchestral use and solo performance. The Arban Method for valved brass instruments is still used extensively and his instructions for double and triple tonguing have become standard technique for brass instrument players.

The Courtois family established two separate brass companies, involving many relatives for several generations, but it is the one managed by Antoine from 1844-1880 that has persisted under the direction of three generations of the Gaudet family since 1917 and kept the original name and maintained the company's reputation for high quality and limited production. In museums and private collections throughout the world, the large number and variety of Courtois instruments indicate that no design or fabrication task was beyond the capability of this company. Saxhorns, slide trumpets and trombones, stolzel and rotary cornets, circular cornets and many other distinctive types of instruments in collections carry the Courtois label. Courtois instruments today are among the most popular imports. The U.S. distributor for Courtois instruments in G. Leblanc Corporation of Kenosha, Wisconsin.

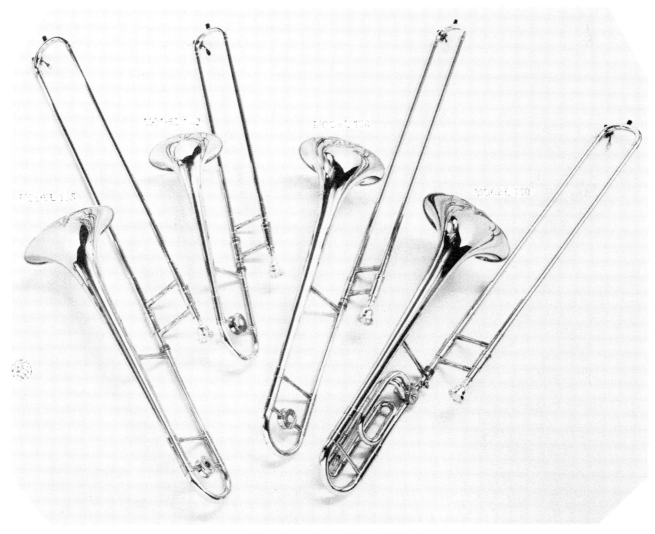

Courtois trombones *(Courtois photo)*

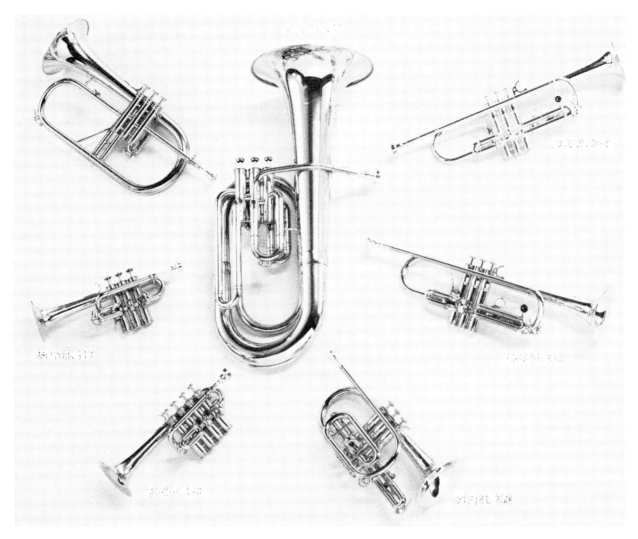

Courtois trumpets, cornet, flugelhorn and baritone horn
(Courtois photo)

Some Courtois trumpets and flugelhorns are designed so that the vibrating air column goes straight through the valve assembly to eliminate the seven curved passages that are found in all other valve designs including rotaries. This reduces turbulence and greatly improves the tone quality and responsiveness of these models. This design was used by Gautrot and probably other makers as early as 1860. Courtois does not claim credit for this invention but is one of the few makers currently using it.

DIRECT-AIR PRINCIPLE

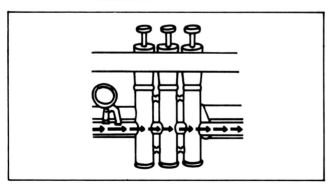

Four new Courtois trumpets in key of C. *(Courtois photo)*

DEG Music Products was established by Donald E. Getzen in 1964 after the Getzen Company, founded in 1939 by his father, T. J. Getzen, was sold to Harold M. Knowlton. The Getzen Company was originally a wholesale rebuilding and repair service for music dealers throughout the country and that function was transferred to a new corporation in Elkhorn, Wisconsin, organized by another of T. J. Getzen's sons, Robert, as Allied Music Corporation. Allied Music is now one of the largest repair and rebuilding shops in the world, with a record of restoring over 200,000 instruments. Robert's sons, Thomas and Edward, concentrated on providing replacement parts and repair tools for the music industry and their company, Allied Supply Corporation, is nationally known for this service.

When Donald E. Getzen began independent manufacture of brass instruments he had the unusually difficult task of having to avoid duplication of the Getzen products and distinctive features which he and his family had developed. The DEG instruments, therefore, have been characterized by additional improvements and a greater diversity of models than are provided by large volume manufacturers. Donald Getzen was trained by his father and brother and has also been strongly influenced by his study of the custom design and manufacturing techniques of Bach, Schilke and many other American and European designers. His line of "Dynasty" bugles provides a full range of integrated tone voicing from piccolo soprano to contra bass and have been adopted by over 100 of the leading American drum corps. Also under the "Dynasty" label, a full line of marching brass instruments shaped like bugles have been developed.

DEG is the only American manufacturer currently offering a gold-plated inner bell, finger buttons and mouthpiece as standard finish on a Bb trumpet (the "Bravura" model). The DEG professional grade brasses are labeled "Donald E. Getzen Signature" with the usual choice of finishes. The "Caravelle" and "Caravelle Classic" models are for student and intermediate players and include all types of brasses. In addition, DEG sells Willson euphoniums and tubas.

(left to right) Donald E. Getzen, President, DEG Music Products; Thomas R. Getzen, President, Allied Supply Corporation; J. Robert Getzen, President, Allied Music Corporation; Edward M. Getzen, Vice President, Allied Supply Corporation; Daniel E. Getzen, son of Donald E. Getzen. *(DEG photo)*

Allied and DEG factories *(DEG photo)*

CARL FISCHER, INC.

The Carl Fischer Music Company was established about 1872 in New York as a music publishing and instrument importing business. For many years Fischer was the sole U.S. agent for Besson instruments and proudly added that information to the already crowded engraving on the Besson bells. The added label, with Fischer's street address, is often useful in determining the date of manufacture of important brasses because Lyndesay Langwill's *Index of Musical Wind Instruments* gives accurate dates for the frequently changing location of Fischer's store until he settled at the present location in Cooper Square about 1882.

In addition to the long term franchise for Besson, Fischer sold brass instruments from many other makers under the Carl Fischer label. Collectors have traced the origins of some of the early 20th century Carl Fischer stenciled brasses to Courtois, Alexander, Bohland & Fuchs and other European makers on the evidence of distinctive design details.

Later, Fischer sold American band instruments under his label and served as a distributor for many American manufacturers. By providing a comprehensive catalog of solo, band and orchestra music in addition to instruments and accessories, Fischer was able to serve as a full-service resource for individuals, schools and all kinds of musical organizations.

Later, Fischer sold American band instruments under his label and served as a distributor for many American manufacturers. By providing a comprehensive catalog of solo, band and orchestra music in addition to instruments and accessories, Fischer was able to serve as a full-service resource for individuals, schools and all kinds of musical organizations.

The Carl Fischer Company is now organized into three divisions—publication, distribution and retail sales. The retail stores in New York and Chicago concentrate on music sales but the Boston store also serves as a dealer for the major band instrument lines.

Carl Fischer label Bb trumpet with rotary change to A

Carl Fischer label French horn made in Italy.

GETZEN
ELKHORN, WISCONSIN 53121

The Getzen Company began as an instrument repair shop in an old three-story barn in Elkhorn, Wisconsin, in 1939. The owner, T. J. Getzen, had been a superintendent of the Frank Holton Band Instrument Company and trained his sons, Donald and Robert, in all phases of instrument fabrication and repair. Since there was no brass available for new instruments during World War II, keeping existing ones in playable condition was a major industry in which the Getzen family played a key role.

After World War II the company began to manufacture student instruments and to distribute some imported models to augment the product line. Getzen was one of the first companies to recognize the tremendous sales potential for piston bugles to equip the large number of drum and bugle corps being organized by schools, youth organizations, American Legion posts and other groups. With this early lead in a new product area, coupled with heavy demand for conventional brasses, Getzen was able to expand into large scale production and sales in a relatively short period of time.

In 1960, the health and vigor of the company enabled them to invest in research and development of new instrument designs and to build a new and improved factory under the leadership of Harold M. Knowlton, who purchased the company at that time. Before the transfer of ownership, Robert Getzen had moved the repair business to Lake Geneva, Wisconsin, and operated it as a separate corporation, Allied Music Corporation, with a subsidiary, Allied Supply Corporation, concentrating on the sale of instrument parts and repair tools. The other son, Donald E. Getzen, founded DEG Music Products in Lake Geneva as an instrument factory and competes in the same markets and all product lines with the parent company.

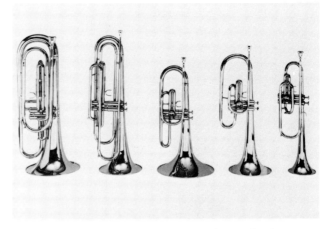

Matched set of two-piston bugles *(Getzen photo)*

The culmination of the Getzen Company's research and development program, with the consulting assistance of Carl "Doc" Severinsen, was a new line of trumpets that found immediate acceptance from professional players when introduced in 1963 and their popularity has increased since the 1985 introduction of an "Eterna II" B*b* trumpet designed for symphony and brass ensemble use. Many soloists and symphony players throughout the world use and endorse Getzen instruments.

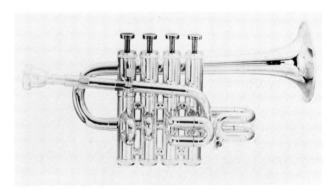

"Eterna" 4 valve piccolo trumpet *(Getzen photo)*

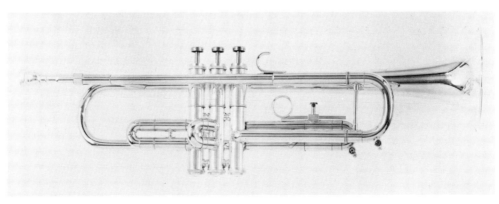

"Eterna" Bb trumpet *(Getzen photo)*

"Eterna" short model cornet *(Getzen photo)*

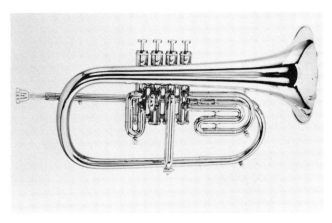

"Eterna" 4 valve flugelhorn *(Getzen photo)*

The most distinctive feature of Getzen instruments is the Amado water key which eliminates the distortion of sound waves reacting to holes in the tubing. The Amado water key is operated by a small button instead of the conventional spring-loaded lever with a cork or rubber seal.

Getzen is able to supply a complete line of top quality tubas through its association with the Meinl-Weston Company in West Germany. Both American and European artists assisted in the development of this line of instruments. Getzen offers 21 different models in a full range of keys, piston and rotary valve types and in three price grades.

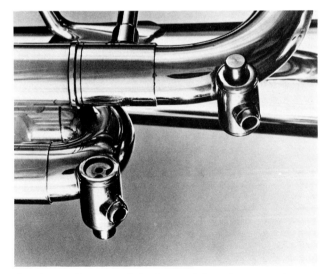

Amado water keys, an exclusive feature of Getzen instruments for many years, have now been adopted by other manufacturers *(Getzen photo)*

Meinl-Weston tuba *(Getzen photo)*

GIARDINELLI
NEW YORK

The Giardinelli Band Instrument Company began as a small New York repair shop in 1947, branched out into small quantity clarinet manufacture for a short time and then began to concentrate more on brass mouthpiece custom modification. This became so time-consuming and inefficient that Robert Giardinelli, the founder, started production of screw rim mouthpieces to give players an inexpensive and efficient method of experimenting with an infinite variety of rim, cup and backbore combinations. The Giardinelli mouthpieces became very popular and as knowledge of their availability spread, professional players from all over the U.S. and foreign countries were depending on Giardinelli to solve their mouthpiece problems. This required expansion of mouthpiece production to as much as 15,000 units per year to meet demands from local customers and retail dealers in the U.S., Canada and Europe.

The professional and advanced student players who were trying to find the best possible mouthpiece characteristics for their needs were even more concerned with finding instruments that would meet their individual requirements. For this reason, Giardinelli stocks large quantities of every brand and model of brass instrument on the market and has facilities for extensive testing and comparison of instruments. When none of the stock models are satisfactory, Giardinelli's technicians are able to make custom modifications to suit the most unusual requirements. This capability even extends to fabrication of replicas of rare and early instruments.

In addition to stock and custom instruments, Giardinelli has been able to arrange for importation under his label of several lines of European instruments which combine good quality with reasonable price.

In 1984, Scheiwiller Mid-State Leasing Corporation purchased the Giardinelli Band Instrument Company along with a number of other large musical instrument stores in the Northeast and Midwest. Most of the sales and technical staff have stayed with the new owners to assure continuation of the unique services provided by this establishment.

Giardinelli three piece mouthpiece permits interchanging rim, cup, backbore and receiver to suit a variety of instruments and playing requirements *(Giardinelli photo)*

Robert Giardinelli explaining custom trombone modifications
(Giardinelli photo)

31

Holton ◀

Frank Holton was born in 1856 and spent his early years as a cornet, trombone and vocal soloist with several traveling shows and a variety of circus, military and concert bands, including several tours with the Sousa Band. In 1884 he established a musical instrument and accessory business in Grand Rapids, Michigan, in association with J. W. York, who also became a prominent brass instrument maker. Holton finally stopped touring about 1898 and settled in Chicago where he opened another used instrument store and experimented with the manufacture of trombone slide oil. This wasn't successful or profitable enough so he branched out into small-scale manufacturing of trombones. The popularity of his instruments enabled him to expand plant facilities several times in Chicago so that by the time he moved his factory to Elkhorn, Wisconsin, in 1918 he was a highly respected maker of cornets, trumpets and trombones. Some of his Chicago instruments are still in existence and compare favorably with the best of the period.

In Elkhorn, he had to build new facilities and train a new group of craftsmen. Also, he was finding that the demand for professional instruments was limited and further restricted by the fierce competition between the large number of very competent brass makers in the Midwest and Northeast sections of the country. As the school music movement developed with strong encouragement from Holton and the other manufacturers, production shifted from the earlier emphasis on custom-made professional instruments to inexpensive mass-produced student models for this new and seemingly unlimited market. By adding woodwinds to this product line at the right time, Holton was able to take advantage of a 1920's craze for C melody saxophones and raise production to an all-time record of 500,000 instruments sold in 1920.

Frank Holton 1858-1942 *(Leblanc photo)*

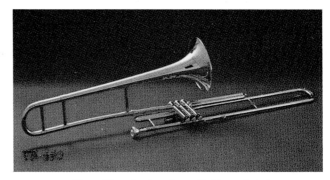

Tenor Bb valve trombone *(Leblanc photo)*

Tenor Bb trombone with rotary F attachment *(Leblanc photo)*

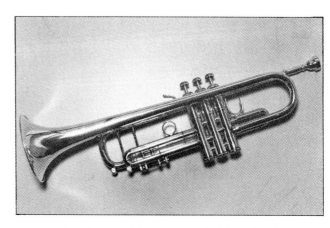

Symphony model Bb trumpet *(Leblanc photo)*

Holton sold his interest in the company to Fred Kull just before World War II and from that time until the end of the war the Holton Company concentrated on military contracts for instruments and other products. Elliot Kehl and Grover Kull succeeded Fred Kull in the post-war restoration of the company to band instrument manufacturing. With the assistance of designer and evaluator, Arvid Walters, many models were redesigned or improved at that time. The best known design achievement of Walters was the development of the Farkas Double Horn in collaboration with Phillip Farkas, first hornist with the Chicago Symphony and more recently professor of music at Indiana University. The next change in management and operations occurred in 1963 with the purchase of the Holton Company by G. Leblanc Corporation, a major manufacturer of woodwinds and distributor of the (Paris) Leblanc, Courtois and Noblet instruments.

Modern Holton brasswinds consist of a full line of marching and concert band instruments and also include some with highly unique features developed at the request of individual players with unusual requirements and later incorporated into stock model production. In addition to the Tuckwell and the Farkas double horns, there is an Al Hirt model trumpet, a quarter tone trumpet with four valves designed for Don Ellis and a group of three instruments designed for Maynard Ferguson—a B♭ tenor trombone with three valves and a full slide, a B♭ trumpet with tilt bell and a four-position slide in addition to the conventional three valves, and a custom-designed "M.F. 2" trumpet in large bore with enormous power and impressive high register.

Seven inch long pocket cornet with the same pitch and sounding length (51.57″) as a full-sized cornet *(Leblanc photo)*

Four valve quarter tone trumpet *(Leblanc photo)*

"Farkas" model double French horn *(Leblanc photo)*

33

Winfried Rapp, Norbert Boepple and Anton Jillich with JBS instruments at 1988 New York Brass Conference exhibit. *(JBS photo)*

JBS

The founder and president of the JBS Instrument Company, Norbert Boepple, worked for 20 years as a master craftsman and trainer of apprentices at the Barth Instrument Company in Stuttgart. The Barth Company is the successor to the legendary Schediwy Company of Ludwigsburg, founded in 1875 by Franz Schediwy who was an internationally famous 19th century French hornist and pioneer designer of valved brasses.

In 1975 Boepple formed a partnership with Anton Jillich, a professional trumpet player and designer, to develop a new line of brass instruments with design and production refinements previously unknown to the industry. Among their achievements are a unique tuning bell and bell-changing mechanism and an adjustable mouthpiece receiver that permits infinite variations in the gap to allow for individual preference in resistance, volume and tone color. Less visible but equally impressive performance characteristics resulted from their seven year pre-production analysis and evaluation of existing brands. Instead of the trial and error mixture of assorted brand bells and leadpipes used to customize trumpets by many players, Boepple and Jillich integrated the best features of existing instruments and their own innovations into new composite models. In 1987 Winfried Rapp, an experienced instrument maker from the Barth Company and professional trombonist, joined the company to assist with the development of trombones with distinctive features that will rival the trumpet line.

The JBS flugelhorn design uses horizontal valve slides with underslung hook and ring for intonation control. This model has extended valve casings for a comfortable grip with easy access to the slide controls.

The pockethorn is noteworthy for a design that is very compact with an uncluttered appearance and a better shape for handling than most pocket cornets or trumpets.

Adjustable mouthpiece receiver. *(JBS photo)*

JBS Flugelhorn *(JBS photo)*

JBS Pockethorn in B♭ *(JBS photo)*

The B♭ cornet revives the basic design of the 19th century cornopean with an enlarged shepherd's crook bellpipe to make an unusually attractive and well-balanced instrument.

The JBS valved brasses are silverplated with gold plating on finger buttons, upper and lower valve caps, water keys, inside of bell and flugelhorn leadpipe.

Production of JBS instruments is still on a very small scale and the allocation to the U.S. distributor, Charles Colin Publications in New York, is limited.

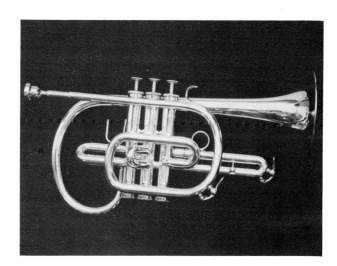

Cornopean style B♭ cornet *(JBS photo)*

JBS Trombones *(JBS photo)*

The first King instrument was made about 1893 in Cleveland, Ohio, by Henderson White, who owned an instrument repair shop and shared the concern of artists of that time with the inadequacy of available instruments. White and Thomas King, solo trombonist in a theatre orchestra, tested a variety of design modifications until they were able to produce a trombone with improved slide action and tone quality. The immediate success of this instrument encouraged White to expand his manufacturing and designing activities. His silver cornet design was distinctive enough to qualify for a patent and of such high quality that it was soon adopted by many of the leading artists of the turn of the century.

His trumpet, alto horn, mellophone, baritone horn and euphonium designs were subjected to constant testing and evaluation by a factory band as well as by artist users, despite the fact that White never started production on an instrument unless it represented an improvement over available models. The King French horn was the first American design to provide serious competition for the imported models currently favored by leading performers. White is also credited with the original design for valve trombone, which was copied by other manufacturers and used extensively by school bands. Recently, the valve trombone has enjoyed a revival among brass players as a convenient doubling instrument in small jazz groups.

Henderson N. White, founder of King Musical Instrument Company *(King photo)*

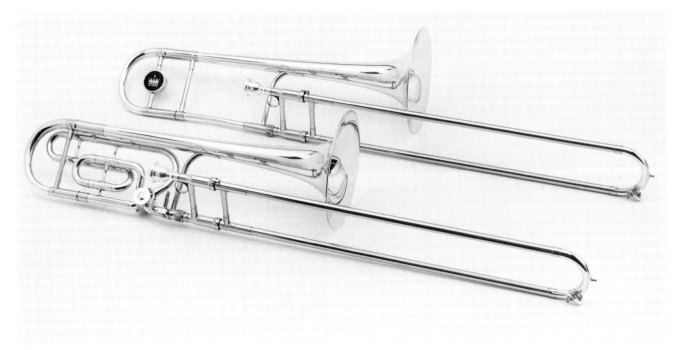

King trombones *(King photo)*

The White Company was not only the first manufacturer to offer sterling silver bells and lead pipes on cornets, trumpets and trombones but is the only American company currently using silver in some of their stock professional models.

The industry is greatly indebted to Henderson White for his many contributions to brass instrument design and manufacture during his 50 years of personal supervision of the King Musical Instrument Company. White died in 1940 and his wife operated the company until it was purchased by Nate Dolin and his partners in 1965. They launched a major program to expand both product lines and plant capacity and in four years had built a new factory, added about 30 new instrument models, purchased the Stresser-Marigaux-Lemaire woodwind factory in France, and acquired an American electronics firm to enable the reorganized King Company to offer a complete line of music products.

Another major change in the product line occurred in 1979 with the introduction of completely redesigned cornets and trumpets, along with some changes in the harmony brasses. The new professional models conform very closely to contemporary trends in appearance, tonal colors and intonation characteristics.

The recent transfer of the Benge factory from Anaheim, California, to Eastlake, Ohio, as a division of King Musical Instruments has already resulted in some changes in Benge trumpets and the introduction of a Benge trombone. The new models are designed for symphony and ensemble use.

Bell front baritone horn *(King photo)*

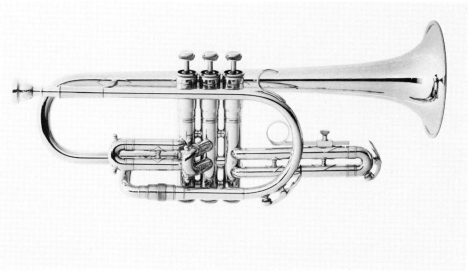

"Master" model cornet *(King photo)*

Double French horn *(King photo)*

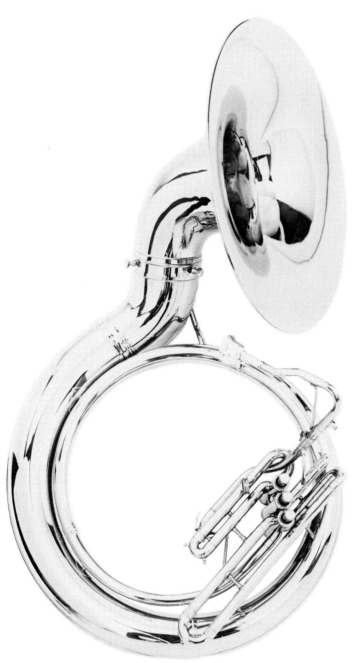

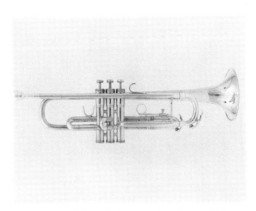

New model student trumpet *(King photo)*

King sousaphone *(King photo)*

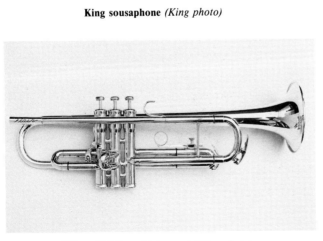

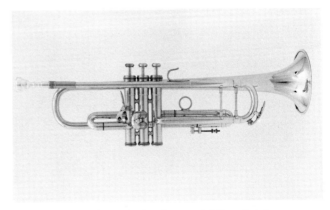

"Silver Flair" model trumpet *(King photo)*

New model professional trumpet *(King photo)*

LebLANC

The G. Leblanc Corporation traces its origin to the Maison Noblet, founded in 1750 as a woodwind factory, and operated by generations of that family until acquired by Georges Leblanc in 1904. The Leblanc family has been in the instrument making business for at least 150 years and are responsible for pioneering work in acoustical laboratory studies that resulted in many technical improvements in woodwind construction and design. The brass instruments sold under the famous Leblanc (Paris) label incorporated the best design and construction features of the distinguished Courtois line plus added decorative details that make the Leblanc brasses more distinctive than most contracted instruments. Leblanc (Paris) cornets, trumpets and flugelhorns are all of professional grade and limited production. They have not been imported for sale in the United States since 1980 but, like other scarce and desirable brands, may be reintroduced at any time.

The American affilliate of G. Leblanc was established in 1946 by Vito Pascucci in Kenosha, Wisconsin. The original purpose of the American branch was to expand the market for Leblanc woodwinds and to remanufacture the wood bodied instruments to suit the American climate. While in Europe as a repairman for the Glenn Miller Army Air Corps Band, Vito Pascucci had studied the Leblanc manufacturing and testing techniques and was able to incorporate them into the design of his factory and laboratory. The Leblanc-designed automatic drilling, boring and finishing machines were adapted by Pascucci to manufacture his personally designed Vito brand clarinets for students.

In addition to serving as the U.S. distributor for Leblanc (Paris) brasses, the G. Leblanc Corporation has imported and marketed the full line of Courtois brasswinds, thereby enabling American players to have easy access to one of the best brands made anywhere in the world. Of even more far-reaching significance to the brass industry is the G. Leblanc purchase of the Frank Holton Company in 1964. This transaction assured the continuation of one of the great names in the music industry and provided financing, marketing and management support for its growth and development.

Leblanc made another important contribution to the musical instrument industry in reviving the Martin Band Instrument Company and providing the resources for Martin to remodel the famous "Committee" trumpet, maintain production of the professional trombone and French horn and to bring out a complete line of "Galaxy" band instruments for students.

The most recent addition to the Leblanc line of instruments is the "Vito" series. Like the Martin "Galaxy," the "Vito" instruments are very reasonably priced and have attractive features for school use.

Vito Pascucci, founder and president of G. Leblanc Corporation in the United States *(Leblanc photo)*

Martin "Galaxy" band instruments marketed by G. Leblanc Corporation *(Leblanc photo)*

MARCINKIEWICZ MUSIC PRODUCTS

Marcinkiewicz Music Products was incorporated in 1983 to produce brasswind mouthpieces with unusual consistency and efficiency. The consistency is achieved with computer generated designs fabricated on computerized machine tools. The improved efficiency is obtained by a less resistant V cup matched to a more resistant throat. To help student players progress painlessly from medium to large cup mouthpieces, the Marcinkiewicz line is made in increments of .010″ in cup diameter to avoid adjustment problems. Although made originally for students and sold for moderate prices, the wide selection of sizes and the design concept has found favor with an impressive list of famous trumpet, trombone and tuba players who endorse Marcinkiewicz mouthpieces.

Marcinkiewicz V cup mouthpieces *(MMP photo)*

As in the case of a number of player/designers from Conn to Callet, collaboration with many other professional players on mouthpiece characteristics led Marcinkiewicz and his associates to cooperative study of trumpet modifications and to production of a line of instruments reflecting these characteristics. Marcinkiewicz trumpets are unique in respect to bore size, leadpipe tapers and bell bead fabrication. There are seven B*b*, two C models and a pocket trumpet currently on the market.

Joseph Marcinkiewicz has been a brass technician since the mid-1960's and credits master craftsman Burt Herrick with giving him insight into the more subtle aspects of design. His skill as a trumpet player was developed by Everett Junior College, the University of Washington and in the U.S. Navy. This qualified him for many professional engagements including appearances with Stan Kenton, Don Ellis, Ray Charles and Arthur Fiedler.

Joseph Marcinkiewicz *(MMP photo)*

ꟽartin ◆

The founder, Henry Martin, learned instrument making in Germany and emigrated to the U.S. where he established a valve-making and repair business in New York. Moses Slater's most famous early instruments with Vienna and string rotary valves, still highly prized by museums and private collectors, were probably designed and fabricated by Martin before he moved to Chicago and worked independently until 1871. After that he worked for the C. G. Conn Company and then helped James W. York to set up a brass factory in Grand Rapids, Michigan.

The company that bears his name was established in 1907 in Elkhart, Indiana, and is still in the same location under the same name although it has been owned and operated by other individuals and corporations during most of its 75 year history. For a period of time the Martin Company operated the Indiana Band Instrument Company but eventually used the name "Indiana" only to identify its imported and student grade instruments.

The "Martin" label has always been associated with high quality and limited production, promoted by a devoted group of professional players honestly convinced that Martin instruments had characteristics unmatched by any other brand.

Despite curtailed production during World War II and the Korean War, Martin was able to survive because of its modest production and strong reputation. In the 1960's, Martin was associated wtih two other companies to combine management and marketing resources in an effort to cope with foreign competition, but it was not until the 1970's under G. Leblanc ownership that Martin instruments regained their earlier popularity.

The Martin line, now marketed by G. Leblanc, consists of the "Committee" trumpet, the Urbie Green trombone, a professional grade double French horn and a full line of student grade band instruments identified by the Martin "Galaxy" label.

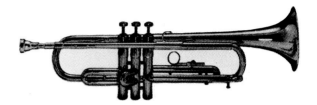

Martin "Committee" trumpet *(Leblanc photo)*

Martin double French horn *(Leblanc photo)*

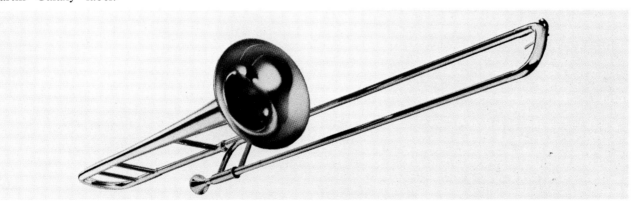

Urbie Green design trombone *(Leblanc photo)*

The Miraphone Corporation, as such, was founded in 1945 in Waldkraiburg, West Germany, by a group of 30-40 instrument makers who left Graslitz, Czechoslovakia, as the Red Army approached. These craftsmen were trained in 18th century techniques of individual design and complete fabrication, beginning with the smelting of copper and lead to make brass and culminating in a custom-made finished instrument. In Waldkraiburg, they started as a workers cooperative, officially registered as "The Cooperative Society of Graslitz Musical Instrument Makers," in the barracks and bunkers of an old ammunition factory and gradually developed into a modern corporation with advanced technology, modern manufacturing facilities and worldwide sales outlets. As one of the most progressive industries in the Inn River region of Bavaria, Miraphone can attact well-qualified apprentices and retain master craftsmen to assure a consistently high quality work force.

Miraphone factory in Waldkraiburg, Germany *(Mirafone photo)*

"Siegfried" model double French horn *(Mirafone photo)*

Bb rotary valve hunting horn *(Mirafone photo)*

The Miraphone instruments are noted for their exceptionally fine tone and this is attributed to the secret formula brass used in their construction. Their designs embody the best features of literally hundreds of years of experimentation and refinements by 18th and 19th century makers. The instrument components are now produced by the most modern manufacturing techniques but the instruments are still assembled and tested by master craftsmen to assure continuation of their high standards of quality.

The Miraphone company now has over 120 factory employees who have produced 450 different models. Their product line has included a full range of cornets, trumpets, post horns, flugelhorns, trombones, French horns, contralto horns, Wagner tubas, alto horns, baritones, euphoniums and tubas in all keys. They have made and marketed these instruments in both piston and rotary valve models but the heavy demand for their unsurpassed rotary valve instruments has forced them to sub-contract or eliminate production of some piston valve models. For the American market they now concentrate on rotary valve post horns, flugelhorns, French horns, cornets, trumpets, Wagner tubas and tubas. The only piston valve models imported after 1981 were BBb tubas and flugelhorns until the recent introduction of an American model baritone horn.

James Gavigan, General Manager of Mirafone Corporation *(Mirafone photo)*

The U.S. outlet for Miraphone products, known as Mirafone Corporation, was separately owned and operated as a franchise by a succession of U.S. corporations until its purchase in 1987 by the parent company in West Germany. Dr. James Gavigan, former national sales manager, was promoted to Vice-President and General Manager of all North American operations. He has previously held academic appointments at several universities as a professor of music.

All Miraphone or Mirafone instruments are professional or custom grade. Some of the cornets, trumpets and other small instruments were made by other European companies and exported to the U.S. for distribution under the Mirafone label. The Miraphone label is augmented on some instruments sold in Europe by the dealer's name and location.

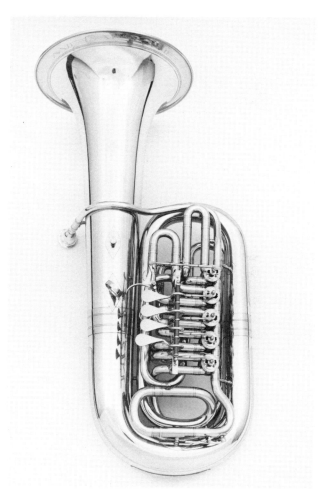

Rotary valve F tuba *(Mirafone photo)*

Oval 5 valve orchestral euphonium *(Mirafone photo)*

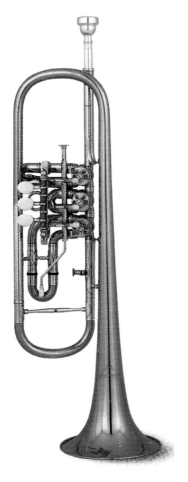

Rotary valve trumpet *(Mirafone photo)*

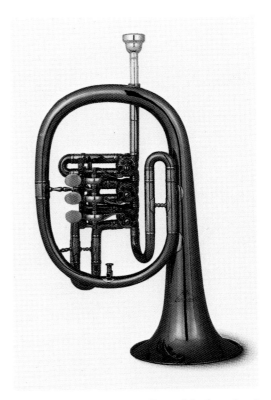

Oval design rotary valve flugelhorn *(Mirafone photo)*

Besson design piston valve cornet *(Mirafone photo)*

Rotary valve piccolo trumpet *(Mirafone photo)*

Monette

David G. Monette is the most recent of the many professional trumpet players like Vincent Bach, Elden Benge, Renold Schilke and Jerome Callet who have gone into instrument design because they were dissatisfied with production model instruments. Like his predecessors, Monette began with repair and custom modification, experimented with leadpipe designs and finally produced his own custom designed trumpet.

The custom features available in his trumpets include infinite variations in stability and bendability, open or resistant, centered or diffused, bright or dark, stuffy or clear tone characteristics. In the technical description of some of the instruments fabricated to order for prominent players, he has apparently managed to combine subtle degrees of what are normally considered contradictory characteristics. In brochures and information releases he does not disclose how these features are incorporated but the purchasers of his instruments consistently attest to what he calls revolutionary improvements in design and performance characteristics.

The first Monette trumpet was completed in May 1983 and since then he has worked out designs for trumpets in all keys and a piccolo trumpet, built prototypes of two types of trombones for testing and made limited numbers of custom designed trumpets adopted by famous players who have previously used other brands.

A complete line of mouthpieces and standard model trumpets is in production and will soon be available for sale. Monette's custom designs and products have found such widespread acceptance with minimum publicity that his new product lines for a mass market may result in a very rapid expansion of the David G. Monette Corporation.

David G. Monette discussing his trumpet design with Adolph Herseth of the Chicago Symphony Orchestra and Charles Schlueter of the Boston Symphony Orchestra *(Monette photo)*

OLDS

F. E. Olds was a skilled machinist and trombone player in Los Angeles, California, around the turn of the century who was drawn to instrument repair and construction by the demands of his fellow-players for help in improving and maintaining their instruments. His home workshop experiments with slide and bell modifications were so promising that he began to manufacture trombones for sale beginning in 1912. The quality of his trombones soon attracted world wide attention and enabled him to expand production very rapidly. Among the design innovations attributed to Olds are on-site tube drawing, two-piece patented bracing, nickel silver slides and the fluted slide.

By the time his son, R. B. Olds, took over management of the firm the product line was extended to include a complete assortment of valved brasses. Olds had the dual advantage of being a highly respected maker and the only one in California at the time so his instruments were in great demand by local players associated with the state's entertainment industry and by visiting artists. The popularity of Olds instruments with professional players and teachers created a demand for student brasses with some of the distinctive Olds features and quality. The "Ambassador" line, designed after World War II and priced for this market, became an overnight best seller and held a prominent position in the highly lucrative school market long after sales of professional grade brasses were reduced by competition from new brands that appealed to the fickle taste of modern artists.

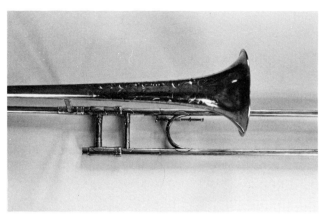

Early model Olds trombone with tuning slide on slide and ornate engraving on bell including standing bear playing a trombone
(Gus Mazzocca Collection)

Modern Olds trombone *(Olds photo)*

Double French horn *(Olds photo)*

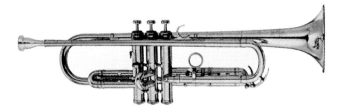

Raphael Mendez model trumpet *(Olds photo)*

In the early 1960's, Olds was joined by the F. A. Reynolds Company and since that time the two companies have pooled design and plant facilities in Fullerton, California, to produce almost identical instruments with separate labels. In 1964, both companies were purchased by Norlin Music, Incorporated, of Lincolnwood, Illinois, and continued to sell under their own labels until production was terminated in the early 1980's. At the time they went out of production, Olds had achieved the remarkable distinction of making over 1,000,000 brass instruments; a record exceeded only by the C. G. Conn Company.

P. J. LaPlaca Associates, Ltd., Barrington, Illinois, acquired sole rights to the F. E. Olds & Son label and have introduced a new line of Olds "Ambassador" cornets, trumpets, flugelhorns, and trombones. These instruments retain many design characteristics of the Fullerton models but boast of improvements developed by designers and consultants at the Shenkelars-Brekoo factory in Holland where they are now being manufactured. The LaPlaca company plans to add French horns, baritone horns and tubas to the line as soon as design, testing and production can be scheduled.

Olds sousaphone *(Olds photo)*

"Studio" model baritone horn *(Olds photo)*

Last professional model trumpet produced in Fullerton with tuning bell

RANSALEAR TRUMPETS

The rapid escalation of brass instrument prices during the past five years has made it increasingly difficult for professional trumpet players to maintain a collection of instruments with ideal tonal characteristics for the wide scope of performance activities engaged in by many of them—orchestral, recording, ensembles, recitals, lead-playing, etc. In addition to trumpets in C, Eb/D, F/G and high Bb/A, as many as three Bb trumpets might be needed by players in these circumstances.

Working together on design and fabrication, Terry Warburton and Ransalear Kay developed a modular trumpet with a selection of five bells and ten leadpipes to fit a single valve section—thus providing up to 50 possible combinations of sound, resistance and intonation characteristics. As a brasswind repair and custom design technician with over 20 years of experience, Mr. Kay was able to produce a selection of leadpipes with graduated bore and taper for special effects and individual preference but with uniformly good intonation throughout the range of the instrument. His five bells vary from the lightweight model with a bright sound and considerable edge to the heaviest gauge model with a very dark unidirectional sound.

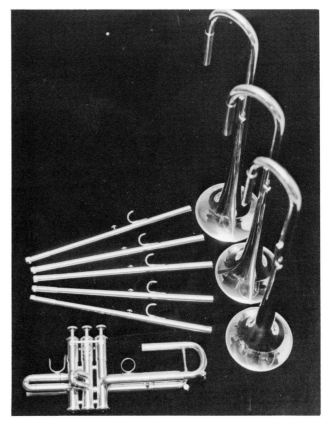

Ransalear Modular Trumpet *(R. Kay photo)*

For some players the Ransalear modular design is an opportunity to instantly create a personalized custom trumpet for general use. Others will buy it with two bells and two or three leadpipes to get an instrument that can be adapted in minutes to suit any performance requirement.

The modular trumpet first appeared with a Warburton label and was marketed by Terry Warburton in conjunction with his extensive line of interchangeable cup and backbore brasswind mouthpieces. His selection for trumpet consists of 46 cups and 12 backbores for 552 possible combinations. Under the Ransalear label, the modular trumpet has been modified and is now marketed by PJL/A Music Products from a distribution center in Barrington, Illinois. Since he has been relieved of marketing and distribution responsibilities, Kay has been able to expand his product line to include mutes, mouthpieces and other types of custom made brass-wind instruments.

Ransalear Kay with custom made baritone horn *(Barrington Courier-Review photo)*

Foster A. Reynolds learned instrument making as an employee of the York Band Instrument Company in Grand Rapids, Michigan, and then joined the H. N. White Company of Cleveland, Ohio, in 1904. During the next thirty years Reynolds became one of the leading figures in the brass instrument manufacturing industry and was vice president and general manager of the H. N. White Company when he left to establish a small company of his own in Cleveland.

With an established reputation in the industry and access to skilled technical assistance in Cleveland, Reynolds was able to experiment with design improvements in his own factory and to produce tubas, sousaphones, French horns, baritones and bass trombones that were rapidly recognized for superior workmanship and accoustical properties. Later, he added small brasses to his line in order to take advantage of the high volume school and community band market. Reynolds also produced professional grade small brasses of such high quality that he was awarded substantial contracts to supply armed forces bands during World War II. Some of these instruments, easily recognizable by the "U.S." engraved on the bell in addition to Reynold's label, are still in use and compare favorably with present-day intermediate grades.

After getting his company fully developed and with an assured place in the industry, Reynolds sold it and moved to Chicago where he did further design and development work for the Chicago Musical Instrument Company, which eventually was sold to Norlin Music, Inc. Reynolds next move was to Fullerton, Calfornia, where he did further consulting work for the F. E. Olds & Son Company. This association led to an eventual merger of Olds, Reynolds and Chicago Musical Instrument companies under the management of Norlin Music. This led to streamlining and sharing of production facilities beginning with the corporate merger in 1964 and increasing to a point where most models of Olds and Reynolds instruments were identical except for labels, valve caps and design details on French horns. Olds had a long-standing advantage in marketing which was maintained independently after the merger. The popularity of their student model "Ambassador" line with music teachers and dealers persisted until the end of production, as did the promotion of professional grade instruments by endorsement of well-known artists. The sales level of Reynolds instruments was maintained with emphasis on the established reputation of the instruments for quality combined with strategic introduction of special features like high-register models, 1st valve trigger and even an ebony lacquer finish option on trumpets at one time.

In 1979 Norlin Music Company stopped production of both Olds and Reynolds instruments but repair and replacement parts will be available for an estimated ten year period from Allied Supply Company in Elkhorn, Wisconsin.

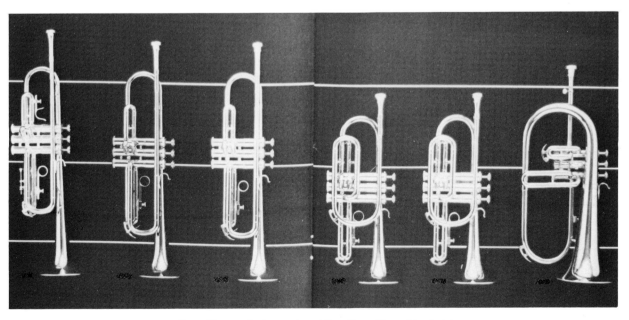

Reynolds cornets, trumpets and flugelhorn *(Reynolds photo)*

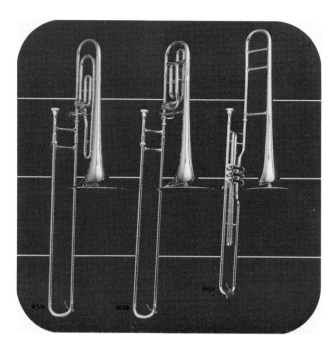

Bass trombones and valve trombone *(Reynolds photo)*

Double French horns *(Reynolds photo)*

Marching trombone and marching mellophone *(Reynolds photo)*

50

SANSONE MUSICAL INSTRUMENTS, INC.

Sansone Musical Instruments, Inc., was founded by Lorenzo Sansone about 1914. He was born in Monte Sant'Angelo, Italy, in 1881 and emigrated to the United States in 1903 to become conductor of the Ventura, California, City Band. His major talent was as a French horn player and he worked his way from California to New York over a period of about 15 years by playing in the symphony orchestras of Los Angeles, St. Paul, St. Louis, Cincinnati, Detroit and New York.

As a member of several New York orchestras and as a horn teacher at the Institute of Musical Art, Sansone was so dissatisfied with the type and quality of instruments available for his students and himself that he imported the best foreign brands of the time for his own use and for resale to other players. He imported both standard and custom models from Kruspe and Alexander until he was able to develop original designs and start his own factory in New York. His designs were intended to correct what he considered to be the three worst problems with existing French horns—muting, transposing and key changing with extra slides. He solved these problems by adding a thumb-operated fourth valve to his single F horn to play in the key of E open or F muted without transposing. This model also had a quick-change rotary slide extension to lower the pitch an additional half tone to play open in Eb or muted in E. His most revolutionary innovation in horn design was a single Bb model with five valves and seven extra feet of tubing to give a four octave range without a key change or transposing. This model also had an extra crook for playing in A. He was convinced that the extended Bb horn would completely replace the conventional double F/Bb horn but it never achieved the popularity that he predicted.

Lorenzo Sansone 1881-1975 *(Sansone photo)*

Single Bb French horn with four octave range achieved by extra valves and seven additional feet of tubing *(Sansone photo)*

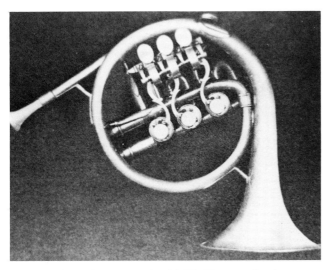

Single French horn in high Bb *(Sansone photo)*

By the end of the 1920's, Sansone had expanded his importing and manufacturing business to include trumpets, trombones, clarinets and flutes in addition to horns in professional and student grades. His top line trumpets and trombones were made by Antoine Courtois (Paris), the intermediate grade trumpets and trombones by a German factory, possibly Ed Kruspe, and he stocked an inexpensive student trumpet imported from Italy. His source for flutes and piccolos was Louis Vanotti in Italy and his clarinets came from the Paola Maino factory in Milan, which had the endorsement of Professor Romeo Orsi in 1880 and still uses his name for a label on all of their instruments, even brasses, although his name recognition derived from his standing as a clarinet virtuoso and conservatory professor.

Sansone developed his own method for horn study, is credited with a number of original compositions for horn and published over 100 arrangements for horn and various ensembles. His publications were taken over by Southern Music Company in Texas and his instrument and accessory business was moved to Los Angeles where it is still managed by his son, Lawrence. Lawrence is now able to devote full time to the business after retirement from a distinguished career as a horn player with the Los Angeles Philharmonic and other orchestras.

The famous ANTOINE COURTOIS (PARIS) trumpets built especially for SANSONE, contain the improved Sansone pistons and slide on the first and third valve crooks or each separately. These trumpets are recognized by the leading professional musicians as the best instrument obtainable. They are easily blown, have perfect intonation and lasting workmanship. A trial will convince you as it has convinced others.

Brass without case	$125
Silver-plated without case	150
Gold-plated satin finish without case	200
Cases from $10 to $25.	

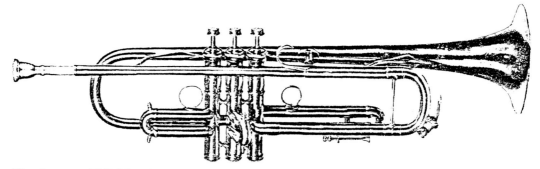

The Sansone "PROFESSIONAL" trumpet, built in Europe, is the most perfect trumpet constructed today and endorsed by the leading trumpetors in this country.

No. A	Brass with case	$75
No. AA	Silver-plated with case	100
No. B	Brass with case	100
No. BB	Silver-plated with case	125
No. 1B	Gold-plated satin finish with case	150

The Sansone "La Tosca" model trumpet is an ideal students' trumpet which can be adopted for band and orchestra work. This instrument is built in two bores, medium and large.

No. C	Brass with case	$55
No. CC	Silver-plated with case	65

The Ed. Kruspe trumpet made in Germany. The latest improvements and excellent workmanship make this trumpet popular in all professional circles.

Brass with case	$90
German Silver (white metal) with case	125

We also carry a full line of trumpet accessories.

Catalog page showing line of trumpets *(Sansone photo)*

Schilke

Renold O. Schilke was born in Wisconsin in 1910 and began his professional career as a cornet soloist with the Holton factory band when he was eleven years old. His association with this organization gave him access to the factory and an opportunity to learn the fundamentals of brass instrument manufacturing at an early age. During his high school years he worked for a gunsmith and learned enough about tool and die making to enable him to experiment with mouthpiece manufacturing on a small scale. In 1927 he began to make custom mouthpieces for all types of brass instruments. His early designs were influenced by the American manufacturer, Michael Getz, and the L. A. Schmidt Company in Cologne.

Renold O. Schilke 1910-1982 *(Schilke photo)*

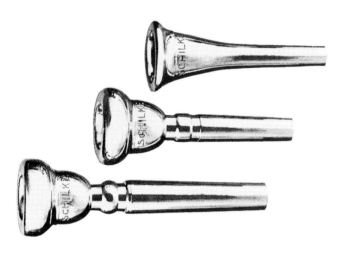

Trumpet, cornet and French horn mouthpieces *(Schilke photo)*

Although he could probably be considered one of the many child prodigy cornet virtuosos of the early twentieth century, Schilke sought out and studied with the best players and teachers of the time. He spent a year with Eugene Pouneau at the Brussels Conservatory and varying periods of time with Herbert Clark, Edward Llewellen, Georges Mager and Max Schlossberg. These teachers prepared him for appointment to the Chicago Symphony as a player in the orchestra and as a teacher in its allied School of Music which became a division of Roosevelt University. He also was associated with the applied music departments of Northwestern and DePaul Universities.

Schilke is credited with many innovations in brass instrument design but the most important ones are based on Mahillon's research with tapered leadpipes and Aebi's technique for locating the source of intonation problems with physics laboratory equipment instead of mathematical or computer analysis. Schilke's technique of charting wave form distortion throughout the instrument and superimposing the pattern for every note enabled him to know what bore size at any point in the tubing would produce the least distorted wave forms for all tones. While limited by the number of bore variations that can be built into an instrument, Schilke uses more than any other maker and can rightfully claim that his valved brasses are more inherently in-tune than any other production models. To achieve the best possible tone quality, Schilke developed the beryllium bronze bell which is supposed to provide better projection with more overtones.

Schilke completed his first trumpet for sale in 1956 and has limited production since that time to a modest quantity that could be hand made by his master craftsmen. In addition to his Custom and tuning bell line of trumpets and the M series cornets and trumpets for intermediate players, Schilke has recently introduced an 'S' series of B*b* and C trumpets.

"Custom" trumpets and flugelhorn *(Schilke photo)*

Tuning bell mechanism and instruments *(Schilke photo)*

"S" series trumpets *(Schilke photo)*

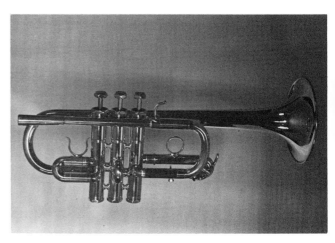

"M" series Eb/D trumpet

The Selmer Company in the United States began as a New York City branch of Henri Selmer et Cie, Paris, which was founded in 1885. Originally, the French company was exclusively concerned with design and manufacture of woodwinds but developed a line of brass instruments after acquiring the Adolphe Sax company. The Sax family is famous for many musical instrument innovations, including the first integrated set of valved brasses to duplicate vocal ranges from soprano to bass. The United States branch moved from New York to its present location in Elkhart, Indiana, in 1927 and concentrated on distribution of Selmer-Paris instruments.

The Selmer-Paris cornets, trumpets, flugelhorns and trombones have enjoyed great popularity with artists in Europe and the United States for many years because of outstanding playing characteristics and unusual design features. The K-Modified trumpet has double-walled valve casings and a first valve trigger, the Radial 2° has radially mounted valves for more natural finger action and the DeVille model is of conventional design. Selmer C and Eb trumpets are very rare but the 4-valve piccolo Bb/A is the most preferred and largest selling instrument of that type in the world. Later, the American-made student grade "Bundy" and intermediate grade "Signet" designed by Vincent Bach were added to the Selmer product line.

In 1961 Vincent Bach joined the Selmer Company as a consultant-designer and transferred manufacture and distribution of his instruments to the Elkhart plant. Selmer provided the facilities for greatly expanded production of Bach instruments while adhering faithfully to Bach's designs and standards of quality and uniformity. Gradually, Bach "Stradivarius" cornets, trumpets, flugelhorns and trombones have replaced Selmer-Paris models in the Selmer catalog so that the only Selmer-Paris brass instrument currently imported on a large scale is the piccolo trumpet.

Selmer (Paris) "Bolero" Bb/F tenor trombone *(Selmer photo)*

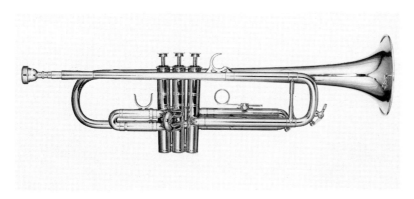

Selmer (Paris) "Radial 2°" Bb trumpet *(Selmer photo)*

Selmer (Paris) Bb piccolo trumpet *(Selmer photo)*

55

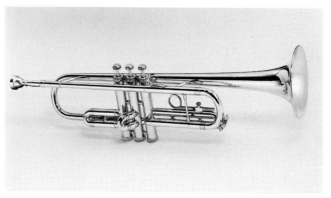

Selmer "Signet" Bb trumpet *(Selmer photo)*

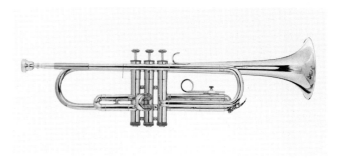

Bundy Bb trumpet *(Selmer photo)*

Bundy baritone horn *(Selmer photo)*

Selmer "Signet" flugelhorn *(Selmer photo)*

Bundy French horn *(Selmer photo)*

RICHARD A. SMITH, LTD.

After twelve years experience as the chief brass instrument designer and technical manager at Boosey & Hawkes, Richard A. Smith started his own company in 1985 to concentrate on "bespoke" or custom tailored trumpets for individual players. His clients include many outstanding British recording, theatre and touring artists. Among these and the best known to American musicians is his long-time associate, Derek Watkins, who has performed in the U.S. with Maynard Ferguson, Frank Sinatra and Benny Goodman. In England he has appeared with Johnny Dankworth, Ted Heath, the James Last Orchestra, the London Symphony Orchestra and the Royal Philharmonic Orchestra. Since Smith is a contra bassoon player and Watkins did most of the playing tests on the prototype, their product line is known as Smith-Watkins B*b* trumpets.

Richard Smith is unique among brass instrument designers because he holds a Ph.D. in wind instrument acoustics, has published many articles in technical journals, is a Visiting Research Fellow at Surrey University and continues his field research by extensive travel to factories in Europe, Japan and the U.S. One focus of his research is comparative studies of production line instruments and their prototypes. Other experiments have dealt with playing characteristics desired by professional musicians. Using this type of information to develop a basic design for his prototypes and refining it further by analysis of acoustical wave form patterns in the tubing enables Dr. Smith to produce a line of trumpets that can be tailored to the most exacting requirements of his clients. Once the correct bore size and bell flare has been determined, an assortment of interchangeable mouthpipes can be tested to find the best match for the individual player. The Smith-Watkins trumpet can be seen and tested in the U.S. by appointment at the studios of the Charles Colin Publishing Company in New York City.

Dr. Richard A. Smith

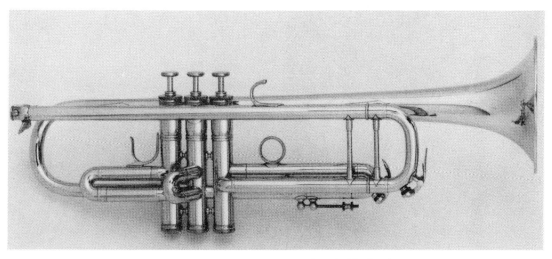

Smith-Watkins B*b* trumpet *(Richard A. Smith photo)*

VEGA COMPANY

The Vega Company was founded in 1881 by Julius and Carl Nelson to manufacture guitars and mandolins. In 1904 they bought out the A. C. Fairbanks Company and added banjos to their product line. The following year they acquired the guitar division of Thompson & Odell. Thompson and Odell also owned one of the best band instrument companies in the United States—the Quinby Brothers factory at 62 Sudbury Street in Boston. That company, under various owners, had been in operation since 1866 and produced a full line of string rotary valve brasses in its early years. After its purchase by Thompson & Odell in 1884 it was known as Standard Band Instrument Company until it was bought by the Vega Company in 1909. The instruments carried the Vega label for the next thirty years and maintained the high standards of quality workmanship for which the parent companies had been highly respected for almost a century. Designs kept pace with industry trends and included the slim "peashooter" trumpet made by many companies and a model similar to the French Besson which was very popular with professional players during the 1930's and 40's.

It has not been possible to obtain a detailed history of the company after World Ward II but at some point Vega phased out brass instrument manufacturing, then the woodwind division and finally their fretted instruments. The name of the company still survives as a division of Galaxy Trading Corporation in California and trade publications indicate that Vega label brass instruments are being imported and distributed.

Hall & Quinby string rotary valve Bb tenor horn

Vega Bb trumpet

Vega bell engraving

Quinby Brothers string rotary valve Bb tenor horn

SINCE 1887 ✹ **YAMAHA**

In 1887 Torakasu Yamaha built the first reed organ in Japan. With the assistance of a friend, he hand-carried the organ almost 160 miles to Tokyo, where he presented it to the music commissioner at the Ministry of Music Education. The instrument failed to pass inspection because it could not be tuned properly. However, the commissioner was impressed and offered Mr. Yamaha a chance to audit a one month music course. With this training Mr. Yamaha built a second organ and, after another laborious trip to Tokyo, was able to get this prototype approved for manufacture and sale. In 1900 the first Yamaha pianos were produced and a mere six years later, the Yamaha piano and reed organ were awarded the Grand Prix at the St. Louis World Exposition. By this time the firm had been reorganized and named Nippon Gakki Company, which means Music Company of Japan, with Mr. Yamaha as the first president.

In 1946 the variety of Yamaha products was increased by the introduction of a line of guitars, enabling the company to serve an additional group of musicians. Further diversification occured in 1955 with the establishment of an independent entity, Yamaha Motor Company, Ltd., to manufacture motorcycles. Despite the disparity in products, Yamaha decorated its motor vehicles with the corporate logo consisting of three intersecting tuning forks in a circle. This design is as universally recognized and associated with Yamaha as the Mercedes three-pointed star and Rolls Royce RR monogram is with their companies.

Another unique music product, the world's first all transistorized organ, the Yamaha Electrone, was developed and manufactured in Yamaha's first overseas organization, Yamaha de Mexico, in Mexico City. Since its introduction in 1958, the Electrone has enjoyed the highest reputation for quality and popularity.

Brass instrument production began with the opening of a foundry and brass mill in 1959 to develop special alloys needed for high quality band instruments. The development of the brass instrument division in 1960 was stimulated by the demand for a domestic source of high quality student and professional instruments to equip the vast number of new musicians enrolled in school programs and advanced studies. Instrument designers were aided by famous Japanese musicians who tested and evaluated the early models and contributed suggestions for improvements needed to make Yamaha competitive with foreign brands. The president of Nippon Gakki, Gen ichi Kawakami, and his senior design staff which included Makoto Hishimima, Giichi Takeda, Seisai Ambo and Yoshihior Kaji were able to translate artist's recommendations into a new line of instruments of excellent workmanship, modern design and superior materials.

To further improve Yamaha brasses, Renold O. Schilke was retained as a design and production consultant in 1966 and within a year Yamaha instruments embodying his influence were shown at the National Association of Music Merchants Exposition. By 1969 Yamaha brasses

Student instrument line *(Yamaha photo)*

Background brasses *(Yamaha photo)*

59

were widely available and rapidly gaining acceptance by professional musicians throughout the world because they combined Schilke quality with Yamaha's lower production costs. Schilke-designed Yamaha brasses are similar in external appearance to Schilke instruments except for the distinctive Schilke hexogonal finger buttons and valve caps.

In 1974 Yamaha opened a new factory in Grand Rapids, Michigan, to assemble band instruments and other products. Since then, the administrative and sales departments have also been relocated to Grand Rapids. The combination of domestic production and imports enables Yamaha to market a full range of brass instruments from piccolo trumpets to BB*b* rotary tubas. Cornets, flguelhorns, French horns and harmony brasses are made in two grades and trumpets are available in four grades—student, intermediate, professional and custom.

Professional instrument line *(Yamaha photo)*

Yamaha "Custom" trumpets *(Yamaha photo)*

YORK BAND INSTRUMENT COMPANY

The York Band Instrument Company was founded in 1882 by James W. York and his brother in Grand Rapids, Michigan. They started a music store and sold imported instruments at first. Later, they began to make cornets, trombones and mouthpieces and to operate a repair service. The company was managed by the York brothers and James' sons until it was purchased by a group of local investors and musicians in 1930. Ten years later Carl Fischer purchased the factory and distributed the instruments from its New York location. During World War II instrument production was hampered by material shortages and military contracts. After the war some York instruments were produced at the Grand Rapids factory but instrument repairmen report that after 1949 York label instruments were made in Italy.

Early twentieth century York instruments were so well made that many are still in use at the present time. They seem to have qualities which professional cornet and trombone players cherish enough to warrant the cost of replating and rebuilding.

York short model cornet

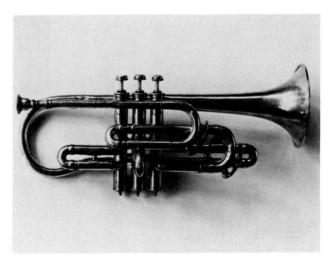

York long model cornet

INDEX